WALKING IN
NORWAY

NORWAY

Alta
20
Karasok
Tromsø
19
Innset
Kilpisjärvi
Narvik
18
Bodø
ARCTIC CIRCLE
FINLAND
SWEDEN
Trondheim
14,15
16
Åndalsnes
Oppdal
Røros
12
13
17
Otta
Alvdal
7,8,9
10,11
Flåm
4,5,6
3
Bergen
Geilo
Oslo
1, 2
Stavanger

Walking Areas

1,2	Hardangervidda
3	Aurlandsdalen
4,5,6	Jotunheimen
7,8,9	Rondane
10,11	Alvdal Vestfjell
12	Tafjord
13	Dovre Mountains
14,15	Trollheimen
16	Sylene
17	Femundsmarka
18	Mountains of Narvik
19	Troms Border Trail
20	Finnmarksvidda

WALKING IN NORWAY

by
Constance Roos

CICERONE PRESS
MILNTHORPE, CUMBRIA

All Photographs, Route Profiles, and Legend by the Author

Trail Maps by Carto Graphics, San Francisco

ACKNOWLEDGEMENTS

Many Norwegians, in town and on the trail, helped make my days in their country special. Some invited me to join them on their walk; others patiently gave directions; many lightened my days with a bit of English conversation. This walking guide would not be complete without mention of my special friends who shared Norway's mountains with me: Dale and Marie Blanchard of Newark, California; Susan Degutz of Staten Island, New York; and Unni Bjerke of Drammen, Norway. Others graciously helped me with the day-to-day preparation of this book: Robert Shankland provided expert editorial guidance; Jason Mitchell helped with translation; professional cartographic assistance was provided by Kris Bergstrom and Story Rafter of Carto Graphics, San Francisco. Kaare and Karin Meland of Bergen offered friendship and hospitality on numerous occasions, and took time to review parts of the manuscript. Other chapters were read by Unni Bjerke, Marian Halley, Kathleen Reyna, and Sarah Roos.

Cicerone Press Guides by the same author:
Classic Tramps in New Zealand

Front cover: Osa in the Hardanger Mountains

CONTENTS

Appendices:

Advice to Readers

Readers are advised that whilst every effort is taken by the author to ensure the accuracy of this guidebook, changes can occur which may affect the contents. It is advisable to check locally on transport, accommodation, shops etc. but even rights-of-way can be altered and, more especially overseas, paths can be eradicated by landslip, forest fires or changes of ownership.

The publisher would welcome notes of any such changes.

Legend

----------   Walking route described in text

....   Additional trails

....   Glacier walk

....   Boat route

————   Highway

————   Secondary road

+–+–+   Railroad

■   Full-service staffed hut (B)

◢   Self-service hut (SS)

☐   Unstaffed hut (U)

●   Private staffed accommodation (full-service mountain hut or other accommodation in villages or towns) (P)

▲   Serviced lodging in Finnmark (F)

○   No accommodation

△   Emergency shelter

░   Glacier

INTRODUCTION

When all the world has grown a bore,
And all your life hard lines,
Come hither! Peak and pine no more,
'Mid Norway's peaks and pines.
An ancient vane

Let's take a closer look at the Land of the Midnight Sun. Norway, forming the western side of the Scandinavian peninsula, shares a common border with Sweden in the east and in the north with Finland and Russia. The North Cape, northernmost point of the European continent at 71°N, lies on a latitude parallel with Point Barrow, Alaska. Norway's southernmost point, Lindesnes, at 58°N falls on a parallel with northern Scotland. To the south across the North Sea lies Denmark. Norway, at its longest from the southwest to the northern tip, extends about 1752 kilometres. At its widest it measures 430 kilometres, and at its narrowest 6.7 kilometres. Its immense jagged coastline is thought to total about 50,000 kilometres long, greater than the distance around the world. This figure includes the fjords and the 150,000 offshore islands of which only about 2000 are inhabited. The entire country encompasses 386,958 square kilometres, 30% covered by forests, rivers and lakes, and 70% consisting of rugged mountainous terrain. Less than 4% of Norway's land is cultivated, leaving 96% as a playground for the walker and ski tourer. The Open Air Act of 1957 guarantees every Norwegian's (and visitor's) freedom to roam in the countryside. One-third of Norway lies above the Arctic Circle, where for at least one full day per year the sun never sets and for one full day it never rises.

The population density of Norway is the lowest of any country in Europe. Most of the 4¹/₂ million Norwegians live along the southern coast, half in cities and built-up areas. The Sami, the indigenous people of the Far North, number about 40,000 and are a distinct ethnic group with their own language and culture.

I hope that this book will encourage visitors to explore the Norwegian mountains. You will find some of the most beautiful

9

mountain landscape in the world. Unlike what you find in many of the alpine areas of Central Europe, these mountains are relatively free from crowds, and few roads criss-cross through this remote landscape. Providing an ideal setting for the walker, cairned routes twist through splendid scenery and link up with comfortable mountain lodges. You will meet a kind and proud people who will enthusiastically share with you their love for their mountains.

A keen walker can be remarkably self-sufficient within this system. Provisions and bedding are supplied at over 320 mountain lodges, most maintained by Den Norske Turistforening (Norwegian Mountain Touring Association) and its associated organizations. Given ample time and energy, you can venture through the mountains of Norway for months without having to go into town for any reason. Your adventurous ramblings will be slowed only by the early swirling snows of September, as the reddish hues of autumn tone the mountainside, and hint of the coming winter.

Equipped with map and compass, you can wander onto other routes and trails toward your night's destination. As some of Norway's mountain areas have had to be excluded here, the book's descriptions are not to be considered comprehensive. This book cannot be taken as a substitute for common sense and good judgement. Nor is it a manual for the novice. Walkers should have some previous experience before venturing out into the mountains alone. Inexperienced visitors would do well to take advantage of the guided tours available. Though low elevation and seemingly gentle slopes invite the eager beginner, she / he must not forget that these mountains harbour all the usual hazards and challenges of any alpine area.

View the jagged spires of the Jotunheimen, climb the high peaks of the Rondane, explore the isolated arctic mountains of the Troms Border Trail, and ramble along the mountain plateau of the Hardangervidda. You can wander for days without a bother, and leave the cares of the city behind. Feel, as I have, as if you are on top of the world. *God Tur!*

TABLE OF ROUTES

Route	Base	Major Access	Start	End
Chpt 5 Southern Mountain Plateau				
1 Hardangervidda West	Geilo	Oslo Bergen	Fossli (Liseth)	Kinsarvik
2 Hardangervidda Central	Geilo	Oslo Bergen	Dyranut	Dyranut
3 Aurlandsdalen	Geilo	Oslo Bergen	Finse	Vassbygdi
Chpt 6 West Central Mountains				
4 Jotunheimen East to West	Lom Otta	Oslo/Bergen Trondheim	Gjendesheim	Hjelle
5 Jotunheimen South	Otta Fagernes	Oslo Trondheim	Gjendesheim	Turtagrø
6 Jotunheimen West	Lom Otta	Oslo Trondheim	Sognefjellhytt Krossbu	Sognefjellhytta Krossbu
Chpt 7 North Central Mountains				
7 Rondane Traverse	Otta	Oslo Trondheim	Hjerkinn	Straumbu
8 Rondane Tops (High Route)	Otta	Oslo Trondheim	Rondvassbu	Rondvassbu
9 Rondane Circle (Low Route)	Otta	Oslo Trondheim	Rondvassbu	Rondvassbu
10 Alvdal Vestfjell (Low Route)	Alvdal Røros	Oslo Trondheim	Flatseter	Straumbu
11 Alvdal Vestfjell (High Route)	Alvdal Røros	Oslo Trondheim	Flatseter	Straumbu
Chpt 8 Western Fjord Ranges				
12 Tafjord	Åndalsnes Dombås	Oslo Trondheim	Tunga	Tafjord
13 Dovre Mountains	Oppdal Dombås	Oslo Trondheim	Kongsvoll	Gjøra
Chpt 9 Central Fjord Ranges				
14 Trollheimen Traverse	Oppdal	Oslo Trondheim	Gjevilvasshytta	Fale

Near Breisjøseter looking towards the Rondane, Alvdal Vestfjell. (Route 10)

Troll welcomes you to Norway,
(these legendary creatures live throughout the mountains of Norway)

CHAPTER 1:

Using this Book

Now shall I walk
Or shall I ride?
"Ride," Pleasure said,
"Walk," Joy replied.

W. H. Davies

This book is organized into two parts. Part I, Helpful Information, gives general details on the book's organization, how to travel around Norway, and tips on Norwegian mountain walking.

Part II, The Routes, describes 20 selected walking routes in Norway, covering the South to the Far North. Many tours can be shortened or lengthened as you wish. Walks are described as hut to hut tours, but it is always possible to camp. The Route Tables provide basic information such as distance, number of days needed, grading, the nearest base or supply area, the closest major access point, and start and end points. Each route description has a fact panel, day-to-day descriptions, and information on alternative routes and access.

ROUTE DESCRIPTIONS
The text gives details on each suggested route in the book. Routes are divided into daily segments, limited by the location of mountain huts. Estimates of both distance and time are provided, although time estimates are the most practical and safe way to guide the walker over projected routes. My estimates, taken when I walked without stopping carrying a 12 kilogram pack, are very close to the hourly estimates found on Norwegian maps. You may want an extra hour or more for rest, lunch, photography, and the like. The distances between points are calculated from topographical maps, and should not be considered exact. Remember that distances can

be deceptive, especially to the inexperienced walker. Alternative routes, if applicable, are described at the end of each chapter.

MAPS

The entire country of Norway has been mapped by Statens Kartverk. The M711 Norge 1:50 000 series, with red and white covers, are the most detailed. Some maps have not been updated since the early 1960s. Since this time, paths have been rerouted, bridges washed away and new bridges built, and roads added. For some of the routes you will have to purchase several of the M711 maps to cover the entire walk.

Additional maps with a scale of 1:100 000 are available for several areas: Rondane, Jotunheimen, Hardangervidda (West and East), Sylene, Trollheimen, Indre Troms (Troms Border Trail), Narvik - Abisko (Mountains of Narvik) and Snøhetta (Dovre Mountains). Many of these maps have been recently updated, although the scale is large. Often only one of these maps will be necessary for your walk.

If unable to buy maps before leaving home, allow time for this when you arrive in Norway. DNT offices (Den Norske Turistforening) (see Appendix D) carry both the M711 series and the 1:100 000 scale maps but are closed on weekends. Several bookstores in Oslo, Bergen and Trondheim that stock maps are listed in Appendix D. Most staffed huts carry local maps although supplies vary. You may find the 1:100 000 series at some larger railway stations and tourist offices.

This book provides maps of each walking tour. DNT and associated organizations publish free sketch maps of most of the walking areas in southern Norway. You will find both useful when planning your trip, but neither should be relied on when walking.

BASE

The base listed is the closest major area where services are available, such as accommodation, food and a range of supplies. Do not expect a base to provide the complete services obtainable in the larger metropolitan areas of Oslo, Bergen, Trondheim, Narvik or Tromsø. Many walks in this book are only a few hours from larger metropolitan areas and use of these bases may not be necessary.

Routes 1-15 and 17 are a few hours' train ride from either Oslo or Bergen. The Sylene (16) is a half-day bus ride from Trondheim. Routes 18-20 in northern Norway are easily reached from the bases listed, and air travel is the most efficient means of reaching the area. However, use of the train, boat and bus services to these northern areas gives you a fuller appreciation of the country and adds to the enjoyment of your trip.

ROUTE GRADING
I have tried to present an overview of each route by addressing the difficulty of the path, its steepness, and its obstacles, such as river crossings, snow, rock or talus. Some routes may be designated as one grading (e.g. Easy) although a few of its sections could lift its rating into a more demanding category (e.g. Moderate). In such a case, Easy refers to the overall nature of the route, and not to an atypical section. In addition, these ratings refer to the challenges of the route itself, and not to its length. Sections are graded along the following guidelines:

Easy: The walker encounters no major difficulties, such as scrambling, route finding, river crossings, talus, scree or snow. Level or gently undulating terrain predominates, and elevation gains and losses are less than 300 metres per day.

Moderate: Ascents are steeper, and gains and losses in altitude exceed those in the Easy category. The path may be rocky or there may be short sections of scree, talus or snow, although no scrambling is necessary. Altitude differences are usually 300-750 metres per day.

Strenuous: This route has sections which should be avoided in poor weather and may have some rough terrain with exposure or scrambling. The walker should be surefooted and unafraid of heights. There may be longer and more exposed sections of scree or talus, and snow may remain on the trail into late summer. Altitude gains and losses may fall between 600 and 1000 metres per day. Novices or parties with small children should avoid these routes.

DIRECTION

Most of the trails in this book can be walked in either direction. If a particular direction is preferred, I say so in the text. With respect to rivers, 'true left' and 'true right' apply to the sides of a river while looking downstream.

TERRAIN/ELEVATION/FEATURES

Elevation gain and loss as well as steepness of the trail are important factors in assessing the day's difficulty. The rocky nature of Norwegian mountain terrain may make walking more tiring than you think it will be before starting out. For each section of the walk starting elevations are given, as well as significant high and low points. A guide to the trail's general steepness follows:

Almost level: Elevation changes are under 30 metres per kilometre.

Rolling: The track undulates without significant net elevation change.

Gradual: Elevation changes are approximately 30-60 metres per kilometre.

Moderate: Elevation changes are approximately 60-100 metres per kilometre.

Steep: Elevation changes are approximately 100-125 metres per kilometre.

Extremely steep: Elevation changes greater than 125 metres per kilometre fall under this designation. You may need your hands for safety.

Special features of each day's walk are described, hazards are pointed out and other particulars of the walk (e.g. mountain views, river crossings, shelter) are listed.

ROUTE PROFILES

The route profiles provided for each of the suggested routes allow you to gauge approximate trail steepness at a glance. Distances used in the drawings are estimates. Note that the horizontal distance on the track is represented on the horizontal axis, and not by the length along the profile line. The steeper a segment as represented on the profile line, the more the segment will exaggerate the true distance between the points it connects. The book's limited page size will make segments of the trail drawn on the route profile appear steeper than they really are when on the trail. This vertical exaggeration becomes especially apparent for longer routes. Routes longer than approximately 90 kilometres have been divided into two route profiles to lessen vertical exaggeration.

SUMMARY TABLES
Summary tables of each route (see Appendix A) provide estimates of how long it will take to walk from point to point along each route.

CHAPTER 2:
Travel Tips

*Here I am, safely returned over those peaks
from a journey far more beautiful and strange
than anything I had hoped for and imagined -
how is it that this safe return brings such regret?*

Peter Matthiessen

GETTING STARTED
Tourist Offices
The Norwegian Tourist Board maintains offices throughout the world. Their free booklet, *Norway,* advises travellers on just about every important detail: passports, customs, currency, travel, hotels, and the like. Specific information on walking in Norway published by Den Norske Turistforening (DNT) (The Norwegian Mountain Touring Association) can be obtained from their Oslo office (see Appendix D).

Passport and Visas
To enter Norway if a citizen of the United Kingdom, the United States, Canada or Western Europe you need a valid passport, but no visa unless you plan to stay longer than 3 months. Your 3-month period is calculated from the time you enter any country in Scandinavia. Your passport must remain valid throughout the 3-month period. Your nearest Norwegian embassy will give you visa information.

Currency and Money
Norway once had the reputation of being the most expensive country in Europe. Price differences between Norway and the rest of Europe have now narrowed or disappeared. It's not that Norway has grown less expensive; the rest of Europe has caught up with it. The total cost of visiting Paris, Stockholm or Copenhagen may easily exceed that in any part of Norway.

The Norwegian crown (*krone*) is commonly abbreviated as NOK. One Norwegian *krone* equals 100 *øre*. Coins come in denominations of 50 *øre* and 1, 5, 10, and 20 *kroner* coins; bills come in 50, 100, 200, 500, 1000 *kroner* amounts. Norwegians round off change to the nearest 50 *øre*. The Norwegian *krone* differs from the Swedish, Danish, and Icelandic *kroner* which are not accepted.

Post offices and banks exchange major foreign currency and traveller's cheques. You will find money exchange offices in all major airports and railway stations. They offer the best rate for traveller's cheques, but there is often a charge for cashing them. Major credit cards are accepted in most places in Norway, and at some full-service, self-service and unstaffed huts.

Customs and Duties
Cigarettes and alcohol may be brought into Norway in restricted amounts. These restrictions are usually not of concern to visiting walkers. Returning Norwegians tend to bring in the limit.

Language
Norwegian, like Danish and Swedish, belongs to the northern group of Germanic languages. A mixed group of the three nationalities freely converse among themselves, each speaking his native tongue. If you speak a Germanic language, such as English, German or Dutch, you will recognize a large part of the Norwegian vocabulary. Norwegian is not a language for the shy; many words are enunciated and spoken with great vigour. In addition to normal vowels, Norwegian has three additional ones: å, æ and ø, which come at the end of the alphabet. Do try to learn a bit of Norwegian, although pronunciation is notoriously difficult for the native English speaker. Because of the difficulty with pronunciation I have not found phrase books helpful.

The Sami in northern Norway have their own language. Sami is closer to Finnish than to Norwegian, and thus even more incomprehensible to the English visitor. When visiting Finnmark you will notice the unusual characters, accents and spellings.

Norwegians must now take English in school, and many, particularly if under 50 years of age, can communicate in English, but only at a basic level. Norwegians will want to practise their English language, but never assume advanced proficiency. English skills fade away as you travel deeper into the rural areas. In some of the more remote lodges, the guardian may not speak English. You'll wish then that you'd learned at least the numbers in Norwegian!

Health
For entry into Norway from infection-free nations, such as Canada, the United States or anywhere in Western Europe, you need no vaccinations nor must you take any special medical precautions. A yellow fever vaccination is required if entering Norway from an infected area.

In case of illness, only visitors from Britain are covered by the Norwegian Health Plan. Ambulance and in-patient care is free; doctor's visits, usually paid in cash, cost around £10. Chemists (*Apotek*) are open during normal shopping hours. In most towns an emergency pharmacy will serve you during closing hours. Prescriptions from foreign countries will not be honoured; you should bring plenty of your prescription medicines with you. Medicines should be carried in their original bottles, or you should carry a doctor's letter of verification.

Time
Norway, like Sweden, Denmark and the rest of Western Europe, is one hour ahead of Greenwich mean time (GMT). Daylight savings time (DST), when the clocks are pushed ahead one hour, runs from the end of March to the end of September.

GETTING THERE
Train
Many international trains connect Britain and the European continent with Scandinavia via Copenhagen and Hamburg. Ferry trains run between Copenhagen and Oslo several times a day.

Air
Scheduled air services from Europe and overseas arrive in Oslo, Bergen, Kristiansand, Sandefjord, Stavanger and Trondheim. From overseas Air France, KLM, Lufthansa, Finnair and Icelandair will route you to Norway through their European hub city.

From the rest of Europe, SAS (Scandinavian Airlines Service) and foreign airlines work together to connect you easily to Norway, usually through Copenhagen. Direct flights or flights with convenient connections can be made from all major European cities several times a day. From Copenhagen you can connect to almost all cities in Norway.

From London, British Airways has flights to Bergen, Oslo and Stavanger. SAS operates from London to Bergen, Oslo and Stavanger and from Manchester to Oslo. Braathens SAFE, Norway's major domestic airline (SAFE stands for the South Asian and Far Eastern routes of the shipping company), has flights between Newcastle and Stavanger, Bergen and Oslo. Other services to Norway from the United Kingdom are operated by Widerøe Norsk Air, Air UK and Dan-Air.

From the United States, SAS routes its flights from Chicago, Seattle and Los Angeles through its hub in Copenhagen. There is a daily flight from New York (Newark) to Oslo.

Ferry/Boat
There are major ship connections between Denmark and Norway, and you can reach Norway by sea from Britain, the Netherlands, Germany, Sweden and Iceland.

Bus
You can travel to Norway by bus from London via Amsterdam and Gothenburg. Other bus connections from Europe connect from Belgium, France, Spain and Denmark. Most regular bus connections from abroad connect with domestic bus services.

GETTING AROUND
Train
Rail travel in Norway by NSB, the Norwegian State Railway, cannot be faulted. NSB links up with bus and boat services from its southern tip to Bodø on the northwest coast. Several main railway lines combine to constitute 4000 kilometres of track. Around 775 tunnels and more than 3000 bridges carry the trains through the mountainous terrain, 76% of which run on a gradient, and 50% on curves.

The main Norwegian lines are Oslo to Bergen, Oslo to Trondheim, Trondheim to Bodø, and Oslo to Stavanger. There are connections to Sweden via Trondheim, Narvik and Oslo. The Bergen Line, considered one of the world's most scenic train journeys, links Oslo with Bergen with an extension to Flåm, and runs 100 kilometres across the treeless Hardangervidda plateau. Connecting Oslo with Trondheim with a western branch to the Romsdalfjord, the Dovre Line crosses the Dovre mountains providing fine views of Norway's inland countryside. The Røros Line connects Oslo with Trondheim via an easterly route through the famous mining town of Røros. The Nordland Line, one of the few trains in the world to cross into the Arctic, runs between Trondheim and Bodø. A rock pyramid at 66° and 67°N marks the train's entry into the Arctic. The Sørland Line links the country's southern peninsula and coastal communities with Oslo, Kristiansand and Stavanger. There are also local and commuter lines in Oslo, Bergen and Trondheim. Buses run in areas where there is no train service; they have replaced the secondary train lines.

In the Far North Narvik is served by bus lines from Bodø/Fauske and not by the Norwegian railway. Railways from Narvik connect with Stockholm via the Swedish railway, the Ofot Line, the northernmost railway in the world. Another Swedish line connects with the Norwegian railway east of Trondheim and runs to Stockholm.

Trains offer both first-class and second-class modern service. For all trains, you are required to make a reservation. Second-class, both clean and comfortable, is superior to the second-class rail travel in some other parts of Europe. You can take a compartment or berth for overnight trips, but be sure to reserve ahead. If you hold a rail pass, you will have to pay a small additional fee for your seat reservation. It is possible to send your luggage ahead to pick up later. When you collect your baggage, you must pay a minimal daily storage charge.

The NSB participates in a range of European ticket-pass plans. The Nordturist pass, purchased at any railway station in either Norway, Sweden, Denmark or Finland, entitles you to 21 days' unlimited travel by train throughout the four countries. It also includes up to a 50% rebate on some ferries, coaches and hotels. Other passes available include the Eurail, Interrail, ScanRail and Rail Europe Senior. Many of these special-priced tickets must be purchased before you leave home. Some are for European citizens only; others are for non-Europeans. Families and seniors may benefit from special rates; off-peak, mid-week or green departure (see NSB schedule) fares can be a real bargain.

Air
Norway enjoys efficient and modern air services on non-smoking flights. SAS serves all major cities. The main domestic airline, Braathens SAFE, covers the country from Kristiansand to Tromsø with modern Boeing 737 jets. Widerøe and Coast Air land at smaller airports in the north and south. In July and August many routes have reduced rates. If you purchase your ticket in Scandinavia, SAS often advertises mid-summer special fares for domestic and international flights.

Car
Driving in Norway is not difficult and traffic is light. Your current driver's licence is acceptable in Norway; an international driver's licence is not required. Four-lane motorways are found only near major cities. Roads are well posted with information and directional signs. Hairpin turns are common, especially in western Norway. Norwegian law requires that you drive with dipped headlights, yield to the car on the right, use seatbelts in both the front and rear seats and never cross the unbroken line in the middle of the road. Laws against speeding, as well as driving and drinking, are rigorously enforced.

Bus
Buses provide frequent and efficient service throughout Norway. Where the train and coastal steamer end, the bus begins. Few settlements are too tiny or remote for a bus service. Nor-Way Bussekspress, which travels long distance routes, will carry you into northern Norway. You need no seat reservations and you pay the driver when you board. It is helpful to carry with you a copy of the Nor-Way Bussekspress timetable which covers the whole country. This does not cover the numerous local bus routes which connect with the trains and Nor-Way Bussekspress. You can obtain these times at local train and bus stations. Buses are less expensive than trains. Holders of an Interrail pass are entitled to a 50% reduction on Nor-Way Bussekspress, but not on local routes.

Taxi

Even the smallest towns offer a taxi (*drosje*) service. You may want to use one to reach walking areas after arriving by bus or train. Taxi stands are often found just outside the rail station. Taxis can be expensive, especially if they arrive from a neighbouring town.

Coastal Steamer

Since 1893 the renowned Coastal Express, *Hurtigruten*, has been carrying passengers, freight, cars and mail up and down Norway's coastline. Flying the flag of the Norwegian Postal Service, the ships leave Bergen every day of the year on a 6-day voyage up to Kirkenes on the North Cape, near the Russian border. The round-trip takes 11 days and includes calls at 35 harbours. For many of these ports, the twice-a-day visits from the steamer (one heading north, one south) are their only link to the outside world. Locals and tourists alike take advantage of this unique service. This trip is outstandingly beautiful, but notoriously expensive, especially if you want a cabin. Deck passengers pay less, and may sometimes board without reservations. Taking the coastal steamer is a fine way to join some of the walks in this book, especially in northern Norway, such as those departing from near Finnmark, Narvik and Tromsø.

Coastal Boat Services

Car ferries and local boat services are an important part of the Norwegian transport system. Among the western fjords, ferries, hydrofoils and catamarans, carrying commuter traffic and cars, serve the western cities.

HELPFUL HINTS WHILE IN TOWN

Accommodation

All levels of accommodation, from world-class hotels to hostels, can be found throughout Norway. International hotels serve business travellers in the main cities of Oslo, Bergen and Trondheim. In the summertime, generally from 15 June to 15 August, most hotels halve their usual rates. Usually the higher priced the hotel in winter, the greater the discount in summer. Except at hostels the room rate includes a large buffet breakfast and the 22% VAT. All hotels in Norway are held to a high standard. If you are on a strict budget, camping is ideal. Campsites, with cabins and tent sites, are located throughout the country. The Norwegian Camping Guide is available from the Norwegian Tourist Board.

Hostels (*vandrerhjem*), meant for youths and families alike, offer a high standard of accommodation with reduced rates for members. Often a sheet sleeping bag is required; some may provide meals and others may be self-catering.

Business Hours
Business hours are generally 0900 to 1600 on weekdays with extended hours on Thursdays. On Saturdays, most stores close early between 1300 and 1500 and are closed on Sundays. DNT and associated touring offices are closed on Saturday and Sunday.

Mail/Post
Norwegian postal services are helpful and efficient. You can pick up mail, addressed c/o Poste Restante, at any post office in Norway. Bright red mailboxes, embossed with the trumpet symbol of the Norwegian Postal Service, are often attached on building walls at chest level.

Laundry
Coin laundries are expensive and can be hard to find, although tourist offices can help you locate them.

Electricity
The electrical current of 220 volts accepts two round-ended prongs.

Weights and Measures
Norway uses the metric system. Weight is given in grams and kilograms, and distance in kilometres. Prices for fruits and vegetables are often listed per 100 grams (*pr/hg*). Fruits such as grapefruit and kiwi are sometimes sold by the piece (*stk*).

Telephone
Using Norwegian pay phones, which take 1, 5 and 10 *kroner* coins, can be awkward. Domestic calls cost a minimum of 2 *kroner*. Phone cards sell for about 35 *kroner*, but the special green telephones they require may be difficult to locate. For overseas calls, it is easiest to use an international calling card, since hotels often add a huge

surcharge. From Norway, dial 095 and then the code for the country you are calling (44 for the United Kingdom, 1 for the United States and Canada) followed by the city code and number you wish to reach. Some full-service huts have pay phones. If calling to Norway from home, the country code is 47.

Shopping

At a store marked Tax Free for Tourists you are entitled to a refund of the value added tax (VAT) when purchasing goods over 300 *kroner*. To receive your refund, you must ask the store for your tax-free cheque and present it along with your purchases at your departure point from Norway. Refunds are given in Norwegian currency.

Food and Drink

Food is expensive in Norway, but there are several ways to cut costs when in town. A substantial breakfast, included in the cost of hotel rooms, can be enough to carry you through until the late afternoon. Bakeries sell low-cost pastries and bread. Cafeterias and other self-service restaurants are informal and less costly than moderately priced restaurants. Many restaurants have a daily special which is reasonably priced. For a large meal it is less expensive to eat at noon. Water in cities and in the mountains is safe to drink. Beer, spirits and wine are extremely expensive due to high taxes. Beer and soft drinks are sold at many full-service huts.

CHAPTER 3:
Life in the Mountains

Il n'est plus beau ni moins beau que les Alpes, il est autre
Louis Neltner

DEN NORSKE TURISTFORENING

Den Norske Turistforening (Norwegian Mountain Touring Association or DNT), along with its associated local organizations, manages over 320 mountain lodges in Norway. Established in 1868, DNT maintains trails and waymarking in both summer and winter, sponsors climbing courses, publishes a quarterly magazine and a yearbook, and maintains a list of the opening and closing dates for the huts throughout Norway. Mountain huts are unevenly distributed throughout Norway, with the majority in the south, and considerably fewer located in the north.

DNT Oslo office provides general information on all walks in Norway, and you can write to them for information published in English. Membership can be purchased at any DNT office or DNT staffed mountain lodge. The main post offices in Bergen, Oslo, at Fornebu Airport (Oslo) and Oslo S (Oslo Central Railway Station) sell memberships as well. Membership offers a 40% discount on hut and food charges. Families or married couples can buy a family membership. Members over 50 are guaranteed a bed at all DNT lodges. At self-service lodges, preference for bunk space is given to members, and only members can borrow keys to self-service and unstaffed huts. Some private lodges and glacier guides grant a discount to DNT members. DNT membership does not provide reciprocal privileges with other alpine clubs.

As many as 50 local touring organizations function in association with the DNT. Information on routes managed by local touring organizations is available at local touring offices. Trondhjems Turistforening in Trondheim manages huts in the Trollheimen and Sylene, and their office in Trondheim has maps and specific information on their area. Bergen Turlag in Bergen handles the Western Hardangervidda (see Appendix D). However the Oslo DNT office also has extensive information on these two areas.

In the mountain areas north of Trondheim huts are usually unstaffed, and belong to DNT branches. In the Far North the staffed lodges in Finnmarksvidda (*fjellstuer*) are owned by the state. It is wise either to visit or telephone the offices of Narvik og Omegn Turistforening (see Route 18) and Troms Turlag in Tromsø (see Route 19) before starting out and to make sure you have the correct key. Information on walking in Finnmark (see Route 20) is obtainable from Alta og Omegn Turlag in Alta (see *Appendix* D). The Oslo DNT office has limited information on these three areas.

MOUNTAIN LODGES

The mountain huts in Norway (*turisthytten*) are efficient, clean, and courteously run. They comprise three different levels of service: staffed, self-service and unstaffed. There are also private lodges which resemble a DNT staffed hut (see details below). Lodges, as described in this book, are located a day's walk apart, usually 4-7 hours walking time. Mountain lodges provide food, shelter from the rain and comradeship, and make it possible to travel long distances with a relatively light pack. Use of a sheet sleeping bag is required.

Staffed Lodges (B)

Staffed lodges, larger than self-service lodges or unserviced huts, some with over 100 beds, provide full-service, such as meals, showers, drying rooms and limited supplies. Food is often transported long distances and reaches some huts on the backs of loyal employees. Prices at the huts differ little from mountain huts of Central Europe. In Norway, however, you usually have a choice of a room with 2 beds, 4-6 beds, or 8-plus beds. In most instances you will have your own bunk and not be crowded into a small cramped area. Food and accommodation at either DNT or private lodges are of the highest quality. Charges are standardized at DNT huts.

Self-service Lodges (SS)

About 200 self-service huts can also be found in the mountains of Norway, and some full-service lodges maintain a self-service section outside the high season. Since you do your own cooking, food charges are lower than at the staffed lodges. Payment is on the honour system. Fees for the overnight stay and provisions used should be noted on the envelope provided and payment (cash or credit card slips) deposited in the box on the wall.

All self-service lodges are well equipped with bedding, kitchen utensils and canned and powdered foods such as margarine, crackers, jam, dried potatoes, soups, canned meats, porridge and dried milk. You do your own cooking and cleaning, and a chore or two around the hut such as sweeping, tidying up, airing blankets, etc. The huts are often equipped with a standard DNT lock but many are not locked during the summer season. Some have caretakers who are in charge of assigning beds for the night and chores for the evening.

Before and after the main season, some full-service huts operate on a self-service basis. One section is left open for overnight stays, and a key is obtainable from a neighbouring hut or from the local touring office. Opening and closing dates for lodges can be obtained from DNT.

Unstaffed Lodges (U)
Characteristically smaller than the other types of hut, unstaffed huts are locked. They are supplied with bedding, pots and pans, kitchen utensils and gas. You will need a sheet sleeping bag. Some walking areas of northern Norway with unstaffed huts not described in this book (e.g. the mountains south of Bodø) require a full sleeping bag.

Private Lodges (P)
These lodges resemble DNT staffed huts in almost every way. Charges may be higher, but DNT members often qualify for reduced rates. Most private lodges accept reservations. In high season I would call ahead from a neighbouring hut, where they will have the current telephone number, and reserve a space. You can also get the current telephone numbers from DNT offices and call before you leave town.

FOOD/MEALS
You can purchase all three meals at staffed lodges. Breakfasts are hearty, with various selections of hot and cold cereals, eggs, cheese,

bread and crackers, butter and jam, herring and sardines, along with milk, coffee and tea. At DNT lodges you can prepare your lunch from the breakfast buffet and fill up your thermos with a hot drink. At some private lodges, lunches are sold separately. Dinners include soup, a main meal of fish or meat, vegetables, potatoes with gravy, dessert and coffee. There is always plenty to eat, with multiple servings for everyone. Smaller servings are available for children and for anyone else preferring them. Meals served at these remote lodges are of the highest quality.

KEYS

You can get keys to self-service and unstaffed huts from local DNT offices and associated organizations, e.g. Bergen Turlag, Trondhjems Turistforening, Troms Turlag and Narvik og Omegn Turistforening. You must be a DNT member to check-out a key, and a small deposit is required. For walks in the Mountains of Narvik, the touring organization has an office in the Narvik Fire Station. For the Troms Border Trail, keys are available in Tromsø and at other designated locations. Call them for specific information.

In the past few years there has been an attempt in Norway to standardize the keys used in all mountain huts throughout the country. This has required the coordination of all the local touring organizations. In the south, locked DNT huts use a standard lock and the key is easily obtained at any DNT touring office (see Appendix D). In the north (north of Trondheim) some areas still do not use the standard lock, but have their own different lock and key. It is worth your time and peace of mind to check that your key is the correct one for the local area. All northern areas in this book (see Routes 18, 19 and 20) have different procedures. At the time of writing, the unstaffed huts in the Mountains of Narvik (Route 18) used the standard DNT lock. Along the Troms Border Trail (Route 19) the lock of Troms Turlag was used. In Finnmark (Route 20) the huts are staffed and open in the summer.

RESERVATIONS

At DNT huts no reservations are accepted, and beds are allocated on a first-come first-served basis. If you arrive too late to get a bed, you will be given a mattress and a blanket and assigned to a common area for sleeping. Though I spent several summers walking in

Waterfall below Stavali, Hardangervidda West
Torehytta and Hårteigen, Hardangervidda West

Walkers above Krækkja, Central Hardangervidda
The keeper of Skogadalsbøen, Jotunheimen

Norway, I slept in a common room only twice. Norwegians are proud of the fact that no one is turned away.

SEASON

As one would expect of a country so far north, the walking season in Norway is short. Although it is possible to camp freely throughout the year, the opening and closing of mountain huts loosely defines the walking season. Huts open in the third week of June, and close in mid-September. You can expect them to be overcrowded in high season, from 15 July to 15 August. The latter half of August is the quietest and possibly the most pleasant time in the mountains, as a chill comes to the air, red hues tint the alpine grasses, and rain in the lower elevations brings snow to the mountain tops.

Some walking routes may still have snow into late June. Walking areas usually clear of winter snows by late June include: Hardangervidda Central (Route 2), Rondane (Routes 7, 8, 9), Alvdal Vestfjell (Routes 10, 11), Sylene (Route 16), Femundsmarka (Route 17). The crossing between Finse and Geiterygghytta in Aurlandsdalen (Route 3) can have snow into July; it is possible to begin from Geiterygghytta (see text). It is best to visit all the other routes described in this book after 10 July.

WEATHER

Summer is short in the mountain regions, but the Gulf Stream and westerly winds provide Norway with a much warmer climate than its northerly location would suggest. Warmer, drier summer weather usually does not begin before the first week of July and continues into early September.

In the summer, days on the Norwegian coast are warm and the nights are chilly. Temperatures in the mountains drop a bit lower, although remain pleasant during the main summer season. I have found the temperatures in the mountains not unduly hot or cold and thus ideal for walking. During the summer Norway experiences more light than any country in the world. There is no real darkness between the middle of April to the middle of August. I enjoy the long days, and I've no worry about getting to the hut after dark.

The western fjord mountains (Western Hardangervidda, Tafjord, Dovre, West Jotunheimen, Aurlandsdalen and Trollheimen) are prone to more precipitation than other parts of Norway. The more

33

central and eastern ranges (Sylene, Femund, Rondane, Alvdal Vestfjell, Central Hardangervidda, Jotunheimen East to West and Jotunheimen South) are drier. Northern Norway can experience long periods of sunny, warm weather throughout the summer. As in any mountain region, the weather can change abruptly and dramatically, and you must travel prepared for extremes of weather.

CAMPING

Norway grants you the right of free access to the mountains, and the Great Open Air Charter of 1957 allows you to camp freely with certain obligations. You may not litter, disturb animals or damage trees or plants. Camp fires are prohibited from 15 April to 15 September. You may camp anywhere for one night, as long as you are not within 150 metres of a building. In the Rondane and Jotunheimen this rule has been modified so that camping is not allowed within one kilometre of a hut, except in designated areas. Near some of the staffed lodges camping is permitted and an additional fee allows you to use hut facilities.

CAIRNED ROUTES/WAYMARKING

Routes are marked with a typical stack of rock cairns. DNT's red T on rocks is a welcome sign during days of low visibility. Signposts mark almost all junctions, but some are small and have stood for many years. Although waymarking in the Norwegian mountains is quite good, you should purchase area maps.

CROWDED TRAILS

You will find overcrowded trails in the Rondane, Jotunheimen and Central Hardangervidda during the high summer season. Fewer people frequent the Western Hardangervidda (Route 1), Trollheimen Circle (Route 15), the Tafjord (Route 12), my favourite areas in the south. Some of the finest, remote and less crowded mountain walking in Norway is found in the north along the Troms Border Trail (Route 19).

SAFETY IN THE MOUNTAINS

Except for the high season in the Jotunheimen, Rondane and Central Hardangervidda, there can be few people on many of the mountain paths in Norway. You should plan your route before starting out, study the maps, know how much elevation will be gained or lost, and estimate the time you will need to your next stopping point. You should not set out without emergency equipment, extra food and clothing appropriate for cold and wet conditions. Watch for bad weather approaching.

GLACIER TRAVEL

Glaciers are located close to many of the routes in this book; a few routes actually cross glaciers. If routes described in this book cross glaciers, there is an option during the summer to hire a guide. Guided glacier walks are a tradition in Norwegian mountain walking. I have not heard of any accidents on these guided tours, however glacier travel always entails some risk. Main risks include crevasse falls, avalanches and ice falls. No one can predict exactly when and where these events will occur. Your responsibility includes using sound mountain judgement, carrying extra equipment and clothing in case of delay, educating yourself to the risks, and choosing only experienced and competent guides. Unless you are an experienced mountaineer, and skilled in crevasse rescue, you should not attempt to cross a glacier without a trained guide.

Several routes described in the Jotunheimen cross glaciers. They include the crossing of the Smørstabbreen between Leirvassbu and Sognefjellhytta/Krossbu and crossing of Fannaråkbreen between Fannaråkhytta and Sognefjellhytta/Krossbu. The ascent of Galdhøpiggen, Norway's highest peak, can be accomplished on a well maintained and busy trail from Spiterstulen or with a glacier guide from Juvvasshytta or Spiterstulen.

DRINKING WATER

Norwegian water is generally pure, and I have drunk from many mountain streams in Norway without adverse consequences. I usually fill my water bottle before leaving the hut in the morning, and keep on the lookout for animals that might contaminate streams.

ALPINE ETIQUETTE

In addition to universal rules of etiquette rarely written down, established environmental practices regulate many of the world's mountain areas. Foreign visitors should reciprocate the courtesy set by their Norwegian hosts, and set a good example for visitors to come. Carry out all rubbish, leave campsites cleaner than when you arrived, and make sure all gates remain as you found them. Avoid polluting streams with soap or washing water. Do not pick the flowers or kick rocks down on walkers below. Since cutting corners on trails causes erosion, stay on the marked path.

TROLLS

These legendary Norwegian mountain creatures, hostile to humans, can have several heads, a hairy tail, only four fingers, large ears and an unusually long nose (for stirring porridge). They vary from dwarf-like to giant-size. Lurking anywhere in the mountains, they are especially given to living under bridges. Trolls are thought to be responsible for any event for which there is no other logical explanation. Fortunately for walkers they turn to stone in sunlight.

DOGS

Dogs are welcome in the Norwegian mountains, but because they chase reindeer and sheep they must be kept on a lead. They are not allowed inside the main huts, and sometimes are provided with their own special hut or sleeping area.

GUIDED TOURS

DNT provides many week-long guided walking tours, with English speaking guides, during the summer months. Tours cover the popular areas of the Jotunheimen, Rondane and Hardangervidda. A few tours visit the lovely areas of Tafjord and Trollheimen, and Finnmarksvidda in the Far North. DNT provides an English language brochure covering some of the tours offered, although it is not at all complete. Their Norwegian language brochure outlines the over 250 walking tours offered in the summer, and an additional catalogue covers winter ski tours.

A WORD ON NORTHERN NORWAY

The mountain ranges of northern Norway boast some of the finest mountain scenery in Norway. Even in high season you will meet many fewer people than in the southern mountains. Though elevations are not high, this is still a mountain environment and the usual precautions should be exercised. The Mountains of Narvik

(Route 18) and the Troms Border Trail (Route 19) wind through true mountainous terrain on well marked trails. The huts are unstaffed but well appointed and cared for, and provide excellent accommodation for the weary walker. Make sure you have the correct key for the unstaffed huts.

Northern Norway can have long periods of fine weather in the summertime, sometimes when the southern areas are wet. The warming Gulf Stream creates a temperate climate along Norway's entire coastline, leaving its ports ice-free all year, with mild temperatures extending eastward to the central mountain areas. Northern Norway's summer days are bright and beautiful, and at their best between mid-July and late August. I heartily encourage you to experience them for yourself.

Trolls greet you at Grimsdalshytta, Rondane. (Route 7)

CHAPTER 4:
Equipment

He is the richest man who pays the largest debt to his shoemaker.

Emerson

Although you need not carry the gear you would need for the Himalaya, Norwegian mountain walking requires the same sort of equipment used for mountain tours in most parts of Europe. It should be of good quality and ready to withstand heavy beatings.

BOOTS
All types of boot are used in the Norwegian mountains; a good part of your choice involves personal preference. Heavy all-leather boots with steel shanks are far too hot and heavy for the Norwegian trails. Unless you are planning a mountaineering trip, they may be more boot than you wish to manage. A moderately sturdy leather boot with some water resistance and good ankle support is fine. Cloth boots are less resistant to water and dirt. In all parts of the mountains you will notice Norwegians wearing rubber boots. They protect you from water but your feet can get very wet from perspiration. If you choose this type of footwear, be sure they have a lug sole. Boots should be well broken in before your holiday. Be sure to carry adhesive and blister care materials.

Trainers do not replace boots in the Norwegian mountains although they may serve in an emergency. They are unsuitable in wet areas, in poor weather, or on uneven terrain. You cannot wear boots inside the huts, so bring along a pair of slippers or hut shoes for evening.

RUCKSACK
Unless you plan to camp out, rucksacks for 7-10-day tours should have a medium capacity, enough for 10-12 kilograms of gear. Soft internal frame rucksacks with suspension systems of lightweight metal that bend to the shape of your back, and with padding at the hips and shoulders, afford the most comfort. A padded, wide waist belt with adjustable shoulder straps helps to shift the load from

your shoulders to your hips. To keep your belongings dry in the rain, line the inside of your pack with a plastic bag or other waterproof material. For extra protection in wet weather, wrap individual items in plastic bags.

SLEEPING BAG
A sleeping sheet or liner is required for all walking routes described in this book. Bed covers supplied are ample, unlike the skimpy and scratchy blankets I've cursed in some mountain huts in Central Europe. Be forewarned that in some areas of northern Norway, especially in the mountains southeast of Bodø and north of Mo I Rana (not described in this book), a full sleeping bag is required.

WATERPROOFS
Waterproofs will be among the most important items for your Norwegian tour; you should be prepared for wind and rain. Helpful features include a front zipper covered by a double storm flap, storm flaps on the pockets, vents under the arms to promote air circulation, closures at the wrists to block out the weather, and sealed seams. Overtrousers with full-length zippers allow you to take off your waterproofs without having to remove your boots as well.

OTHER CLOTHING / EQUIPMENT
Synthetics trap air, keeping you dry and warm and move moisture away from your skin to the opposite side of the fabric where the water evaporates, sparing you a clammy layer next to your skin. For your upper body, effective layering ensures good breatheability and increases your safety and comfort. You should carry three warm layers for your upper body, two of which should be of wool or a synthetic material, with a waterproof on the outside. If you tend to feel cold, carry an additional synthetic garment for your chest. For your legs you will want at least one pair of long wool or synthetic trousers or synthetic long underwear with shorts. Cotton trousers are useless in the mountains, except possibly for hut wear at night.

Natural fibres, like cotton and silk retain moisture and are dangerous in wet and windy conditions. Wool, compared to synthetic fabrics, is excellent against cold, but performs less well when wet.

You will also need a wool or synthetic hat, wool or synthetic gloves with overmitts, and a change of shoes. Don't forget a water bottle or thermos, maps and compass, sun hat, sun cream, a torch (for after mid-August) and a first aid kit. The full-service huts sell handy items such as confectionery, cigarettes, sun cream, blister care materials, assorted toiletries, beer and soft drinks, and local maps.

MOSQUITOES
In early season mosquitoes can be bothersome in the following areas: Finnmarksvidda, Femundsmarka, the Mountains of Narvik and the Troms Border Trail. Numbers are largely dependent on the time of year, the amount of winter snowfall and spring rain, and the temperature. More numerous when it is warm and sunny, they disappear in the cold. By August numbers are vastly decreased. I recommend covering your arms and legs, strong repellent and a head net.

DRYING ROOMS
Staffed Norwegian mountain huts offer some of the best drying rooms anywhere in the world, and your wet clothes will often dry completely overnight. But remember that dry air may damage boot seams and break the treads; leather prefers slow drying. Just wear your boots wet in the morning.

CHAPTER 5:
Southern Mountain Plateau

Route 1: HARDANGERVIDDA WEST
Route 2: HARDANGERVIDDA CENTRAL
Route 3: AURLANDSDALEN

One does not discover new lands without consenting to
lose sight of the shore for a very long time.

André Gide

Few travellers to Norway miss a ride on the Oslo-Bergen train line. Departing twice daily during the summer, the 7-hour journey takes you through forests and small towns until it crosses the northern border of the treeless Hardangervidda plateau. The Hardangervidda, at 10,000-plus square kilometres, is Europe's largest mountain plateau. The Hardangervidda National Park comprises over 3430 square kilometres of scenery. The plateau lies east of Hardangerfjord, south of Finse and Hardangerjøkulen, and north of the Rogaland-Setesdal Highlands.

Man probably reached the forested Hardangervidda at the end of the last Ice Age. Some 250 Stone Age sites have been discovered from around 6300 BC. Hunting, fishing and calving pens have been found as well as elk and reindeer bones. Ancient tracks across the plateau linked the south with the east.

At one time the Hardangervidda was home to up to 40,000 reindeer, the last wild reindeer in Europe. Their numbers are somewhat reduced today due to overgrazing. In the autumn, the reindeer travel east to their winter pastures, and in the winter they travel west to springtime calving areas. They calve in these wetter western areas in May, while the male and young live in the lower birch forests.

The Hardangervidda landscape offers tremendous variety. The

west and south with their heavy snowfall and high mountain ridges are rich in plant life. Along the western border the terrain drops steeply towards Sørfjord. The deep valleys, thundering waterfalls and glaciers of the western plateau combine to make the western area the most enchanting part of the Hardangervidda. On the other hand the central and eastern lake-dotted slopes are flat, open and gentle with little winter snowfall. This terrain is reminiscent of a barren windswept moorland.

The area is home to several rare bird and animal species usually found further north. Flora is abundant as plants typical of eastern Norway meet those of western Norway. Many reach their southern limits here. You'll find the Arctic raspberry, a (some think, tastier) relative of the famous cloudberry of Finnmark.

Five tourist organizations work together to maintain a network of trails, roads and tourist huts on the Hardangervidda. The entire plateau is also popular for winter cross-country hut-to-hut ski touring. At Easter time mountain huts open to accommodate a flood of holidaymakers out to enjoy the early spring daylight. Summertime brings out a good many more.

TRANSPORT
The Oslo-Bergen train line crosses the northern Hardangervidda (Routes 1 and 2) and stops at Geilo, a good base for this area. Geilo is best known for its downhill skiing, and you'll see several lifts from the railway station. The town offers a tourist office, hotels, a hostel, and adequate supply stores. You can catch a bus on the E7 road that follows a scenic route along the Hardangervidda. The bus stops at several points of entry into the Hardangervidda: Haugastøl, Fagerheim, Halne, Dyranut, Liseth, Fossli, Eidfjord, Kinsarvik (ferry connections to Bergen) and Odda.

The Aurlandsdalen walk (Route 3) begins from the railway station at Finse. There is no road to Finse and you can reach this small bustling winter ski centre and summer mountain area only by rail. If early snow blocks your route out of Finse it is possible to take a bus to Geiterygghytta (see text). The bus also stops at Steinbergdalen and Østerbø. At the end of your tour, there is a summer bus stop in Vassbygdi from where you can return to Geilo or connect to Flåm. From Flåm you can catch the famous train to Myrdal which connects to the Oslo-Bergen train line.

Route 1: HARDANGERVIDDA WEST

Route 1 Hardangervidda West starts from Fossli, where you can visit the waterfall, Vøringsfossen. The falls were discovered at the end of the nineteenth century, when the wild country and scenery of Norway were just beginning to be noticed. It is felt that the discovery of Vøringsfossen paved the way for the beginning of the appreciation of the country's natural beauty and the recognition of tourism in Norway. Vøringsfossen remains one of the country's most spectacular waterfalls. For a country of many waterfalls, this is tribute indeed. The Fossli Hotel occupies the site just above the cliff and provides the most dramatic view of the falls. According to legend, Vøring, a tourist in the area, was travelling on skis in heavy snow across the Hardangervidda. Undeterred by the roar ahead, he plunged into the waterfall's precipice.

This classic route is best walked from east to west. You start with a visit to Vøringsfossen, and end with a long downhill from Stavali into Kinsarvik. If walking in the opposite direction the long downhill becomes a demanding climb.

Distance:	74 kilometres
Time:	4-5 days
Rating:	Moderate
Maps:	1315 I Ullensvang, 1415 III Hårteigen, 1415 IV Eidfjord
	1:100 000 Hardangervidda Vest
Start Altitude:	Fossli, 670 metres
Highest Point:	Above Torehytta, 1430 metres
Base:	Geilo
Major Access:	Oslo/Bergen

FOSSLI (670m) to HEDLO (945m) via BELOW FLJOTDALS (1200m)
4 hours 55 minutes, 19 kilometres
Elevation:	Gradual, moderate
Features:	Waterfall, plateau views, bus (Fossli)

Take the bus along the E7 to the Fossli Hotel. Near the hotel,

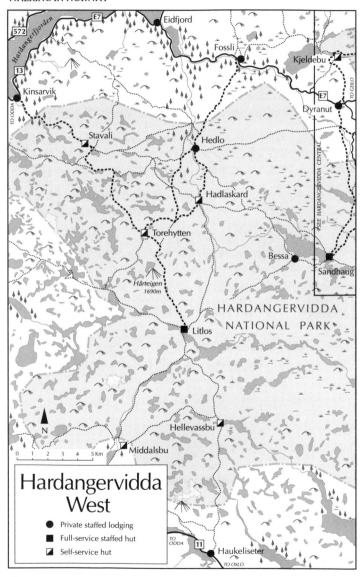

Hardangervidda West

● Private staffed lodging

■ Full-service staffed hut

◪ Self-service hut

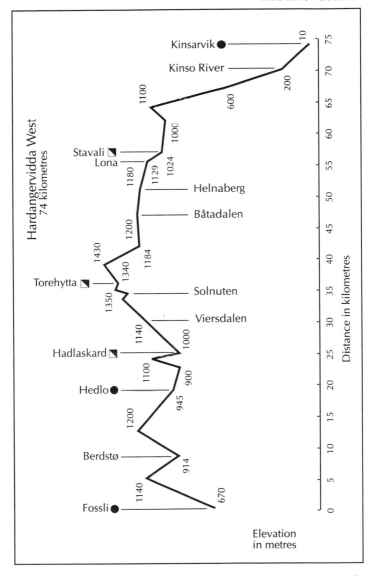

Vøringsfossen drops 182 metres off a cliff, crashing into the Måbødalen below. If you wish to spend the night the Liseth Hut is a 10 minute walk east from the hotel. If you take the bus to the next stop about 5 minutes beyond the hotel, the walk to the trail is shorter. The waterfall can be viewed from here as well.

From the waterfall stop on the E7, walk on the road 500 metres east to a small bridge. Though the bridge is marked 'private', walkers are permitted. Follow the signs to Hedlo. The path may be difficult to follow, so watch closely for the signs. Walk to the west of the house after crossing over the bridge and follow the red Ts through the trees until you join the main track. The track from Liseth joins from the north, and now your route is obvious. As you gradually gain elevation, there are fine views north back to the dam and wide open glaciers. In one hour you'll pass a farm at Skissete. Continue westwards and upwards along the creek for 5 minutes. Turning south and passing above the river below, you gain more elevation to the high point below Hallingehaugane at 1140 metres. A one hour gradual descent follows to Berastøten, where there are several summer homes and fantastic views to the Hjølmodalen cliffs. Cross the bridge about 5 minutes downstream from the homes, and follow the signs to Hedlo straight up the hill by the creek. From the top ridge you will enjoy expansive views of the entire Hardangervidda and of the famous Hårteigen. This mountain, shaped like a top hat, is a major feature in many pictures of this area. From the top descend to the next river bed, and you see several homes on the opposite side of the river. Cross the river on the bridge, and follow signposts east through the rocky gap for 15 minutes to the private hut Hedlo (P/50).

HEDLO (945m) to HADLASKARD (1000m) via HIGH POINT (1100m)
2 hours 30 minutes, 6 kilometres

Elevation:	Almost level, parts moderate
Features:	River views

This very pleasant route to Torehytten can be walked in one moderate day or split into two leisurely ones. Many walkers bound for Torehytten head east from Hedlo, crossing the bridge located

250 metres upstream, continue south to Fagerli, and then walk up the river valley to Viersdalen. The route I've described here, which goes directly south to Viersdalen from Hedlo, is longer but more scenic.

From Hedlo proceed gradually upstream on the river's true left. In warm weather the wide river affords good swimming spots. After one hour you'll pass some buildings, and begin a moderate ascent around some steep cliffs. You'll reach the top in 40 minutes and get fine views of the broad river valley. Twenty minutes more brings you gradually down to the river again, past some homes, and after another 40 minutes along the flat river valley you arrive at the hut at Hadlaskard (SS/34). This pleasant hut was refurbished a few years ago and has a summer warden. You may wish to relax here for the rest of the day or move on to Torehytten.

HADLASKARD (1000m) to TOREHYTTEN (1340m)
3 hours, 6 kilometres

Elevation:	Moderate
Features:	River crossing, permanent snow crossing, waterfall, peak climb (optional)

From Hadlaskard your tour encounters many ups and downs, with little aggregate elevation change. In 1$^{1/2}$ hours you reach Viersdalen at 1140 metres, an old summer farm with distant views of Hårteigen. If you wish to climb Hårteigen continue south without crossing the river. For the more direct route to Torehytten head east across the river at the T near the cottages, to the river's true left. This junction is not signed and there is no bridge, but the crossing is easy. After that, continue east about 300 metres to next river bank. You can cross at the easiest location, or look for the Ts. Walk up the valley until you hit the main trail, continuing east. To the south the large River Sandhaugo appears. One hour from the river crossing you gain some elevation and climb the side of a cliff just before coming upon a thunderous waterfall. The trail turns south-east here and passes close to the splendid deafening river. Several small lakes lie to the south, as you steeply climb above the river and pass through a rocky gap under Solnuten. Your route then opens up above Lake 1268. Ahead you see a canyon with an inlet into the lake. Walk above the lake for 10 minutes, crossing several streams which drain into the lake. You may find some snow on your final 30 minute ascent to a high point 5 minutes above Torehytten (SS/22). These two huts are splendidly placed on the icy lake's edge with fine views of Hårteigen.

TOREHYTTEN (1340m) to STAVALI (1024m) via HIGH POINT (1430m)
5 hours 20 minutes, 21 kilometres

Elevation: Moderate and gradual

From the hut, head north-west on the track towards Stavali, climbing to the high point in 20 minutes. For the next several hours the track undulates above wide river valleys to the south. One hour from the hut you pass far above the huge Lake 1184, traversing large snow sections. There is no hope of dry feet today. Two more hours brings you to the eastern shore of Lake Holma. A good lunch spot lies along the large stream that empties into the lake. After lunch you continue northward and in $1/2$ hour pass the trail to Hadlaskard, which meets you from the east. Turn west at the junction and in $1^{1}/2$ hours you come to the farm at Helnaberg. As you head north, a delightful part of the day awaits you. You walk up and down on the hillsides with gorgeous views of the lakes to the south. Climb gradually to the obvious gap and descend steeply over snow to Lake Lona (1129m). Follow the rocky path for 15 minutes along the lake's western shore to the self-service hut at Stavali (SS/36).

STAVALI (1024m) to KINSARVIK (10m)
5 hours, 17 kilometres

Elevation: Parts extremely steep, steep, moderate, gradual
Features: Ferry and bus service (Kinsarvik), waterfall

From Stavali walk on a moderate uphill around Randinoten and in one hour join a series of lakes. Another moderate uphill for 15 minutes brings you to Vierdalen; a very steep downhill follows to reach the River Kinso. Your extremely steep descent on rock can be slippery when wet. Hope it's not raining. You soon have views of the tremendous two-tiered waterfall, impressive even on a misty day. This is one of the few large waterfalls in Norway not harnessed for hydroelectric power. Continue onward on a 20 minute flat section until you enter the trees. Another steep downhill over roots and leaves follows; it may seem just as treacherous as your first descent. Finally your route flattens out in a wet forest; the going remains rocky. You can now gain views of the third magnificent waterfall, the widest and largest of all. Join the road in 10 minutes and walk downhill along the road for one hour into Kinsarvik.

Route 2: HARDANGERVIDDA CENTRAL

This classic walk is very popular with Norwegians in both summer and winter, and therefore is included here. It is easily accessible from the main population centres of Oslo and Bergen, but you will find it much less scenic than the Western Hardangervidda. However, you can connect to the western area from Sandhaug. This route passes through flat, open country with few distinguishing landmarks and a certain monotony of character.

Distance:	75.5 kilometres
Time:	5 days
Rating:	Easy
Maps:	1415 I Bjoreio, 1415 II Nordmannslågen, 1515 IV Hein 1:100 000 Hardangervidda Vest and Hardangervidda Øst
Start Altitude:	Dyranut, 1240 metres
Highest Point:	Below Langhaugen, 1300 metres
Base:	Geilo
Major Access:	Oslo/Bergen

DYRANUT (1240m) to SANDHAUG (1252m)
6 hours, 23 kilometres

Elevation:	Rolling
Features:	Bus (Dyranut)

From the bus stop at the hotel at Dyranut (P/35) head south, picking

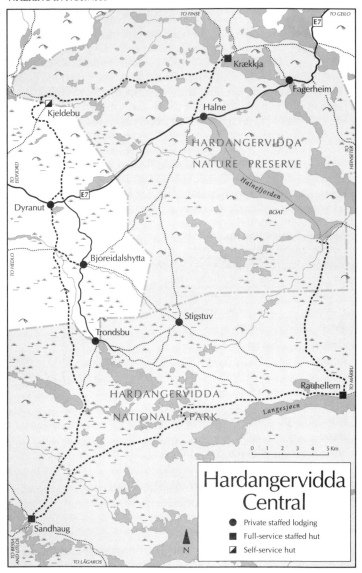

TO FINSE
TO GEILO
E7

Krækkja

Fagerheim

Kjeldebu

Halne

TO EIDFJORD

HARDANGERVIDDA

NATURE PRESERVE

Halnefjorden

TO HEINSETER

E7

Dyranut

BOAT

TO HEDLO

Bjøreidalshytta

Stigstuv

Trondsbu

Rauhellern

TO MÅRBU

HARDANGERVIDDA

NATIONAL PARK

Langesjøen

0 1 2 3 4 5 Km

TO BESSA AND LITLOS

Sandhaug

TO LÅGAROS

N

Hardangervidda
Central

● Private staffed lodging

■ Full-service staffed hut

◪ Self-service hut

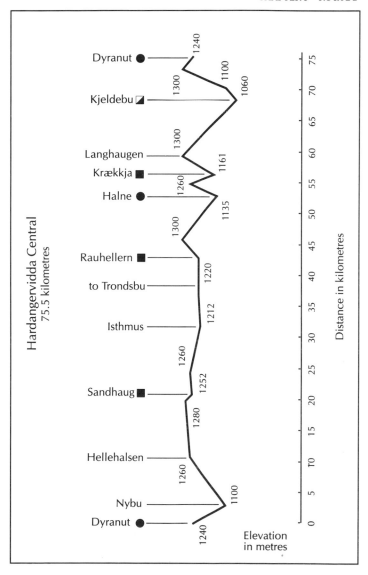

Hardangervidda Central
75.5 kilometres

Dyranut ● — 1240
Kjeldebu ◪ — 1300 / 1100 / 1060
Langhaugen — 1300 / 1161
Krækkja ■ — 1260
Halne ● — 1135
Rauhellern ■ — 1300 / 1220
to Trondsbu — 1212
Isthmus — 1260 / 1252
Sandhaug ■ — 1280
Hellehalsen — 1260
Nybu — 1100
Dyranut ● — 1240

Elevation
in metres

Distance in kilometres

75 70 65 60 55 50 45 40 35 30 25 20 15 10 5 0

up the T just west of Lake 1222. An hour brings you to the buildings at Nybu, and you cross the river on a bridge. Here a turn west will take you to Hedlo (see Route 1 Hardangervidda West). A turn east brings you to Bjoreidalshytta (P/38), a good place to break if you've arrived on the late bus. Continue south on the rolling plateau for 2 hours to Hellehalsen. You can see the road to the east, which goes from just east of Dyranut to beyond Trondsbu (P/15). The large Lake 1223 becomes visible in the west. This featureless flat moorland, with few landmarks and its cold western winds, is very typical of the central and eastern Hardangervidda.

Past the summer homes at Hellehalsen, a dirt road becomes part of the track for 3 kilometres. Continuing south you pass numerous ponds and lakes until you approach the western mountain ridge of Trondavadnutane, which offers the first break from the winds. Gradually you drop down to Sandhaug (B/80), a large DNT lodge with excellent food. This winter ski centre is nicely situated with fine views of the mountains and surrounding lakes.

SANDHAUG (1252m) to RAUHELLERN (1220m)
7 hours, 22 kilometres

Elevation: Almost level

From Sandhaug follow the signs north-east to Rauhellern. Your entire day is level with occasional views of ridges to the north. The middle of your day finds you crossing an isthmus to Lake 1212. You then begin the long trudge on the northern edge of Langesjøen. Your night's destination Rauhellern (B/65) can be spotted from a distance of about 5 kilometres, still about 2 hour's walk away.

RAUHELLERN (1220m) to HALNE (1135m) via HIGH POINT (1260m)
3 hours 30 minutes, 10 kilometres

Elevation: Almost level
Features: Boat service, bus, cafeteria (Halne)

From Rauhellern head north, south of the mountain ridge, gradually rising to a high point under the peak. The expansive scenery varies little as you cross Skyttarbudalen to reach Halnefjorden. The boat service is offered during the summer only and can be erratic; be sure to ask at the hut whether the boat is running. The boat docks on the east side of the E7, a few minutes from private accommodation at Halne (P/65).

HALNE (1135m) to KRÆKKJA (1161m)
1 hour 20 minutes, 3.5 kilometres

Elevation:	Moderate
Features:	Hardangervidda views, boat service, bus, cafeteria (Halne)

From Halne walk one kilometre west on the E7 to the signs to Krækkja. Turn north and ascend on the true right of the stream to the top at 1268 metres. There are outstanding views to the north. In a few minutes you pass tomorrow's turnoff west to Kjeldebu. Turn north-east at the junction and the trail goes slowly downhill in 15 minutes to the hut Krækkja (B/85) on the lake's edge.

KRÆKKJA (1161m) to KJELDEBU (1060m) via LANGHAUGEN (1300m)
4 hours, 12 kilometres

Elevation:	Moderate, rolling

From Krækkja backtrack from yesterday's route up the hill to the turnoff to Halne. Head west and continue to climb to the high plateau until you pass between Langhaugen (1346m) and Lake 1263. This is a lovely high mountain lake basin with fine views in all directions. Pass slowly down through the pleasant valley until you reach the River Kjeldo valley. It is possible to see your final destination Kjeldebu (SS/40) and you may be able to cross the south side of Lake 1055, a more direct route to the hut. You will be assisted by low water, long legs, and a bit of luck. Otherwise you must pass north of the lake and proceed around the lake's west side and over a summer bridge to the hut (not marked on the 1415 I Bjoreio map).

KJELDEBU (1060m) to DYRANUT (1240m)
3 hours, 7 kilometres

Elevation:	Moderate
Features:	Bus and cafeteria (Dyranut)

From the hut follow the cairns south (not marked on map 1415 I Bjoreio) to the river basin. After 1½ kilometres you pick up the old track. At first you have many short ups and downs, then after crossing the river you rise slowly to a point below the hill Dyranutane. The path follows slowly around its base and in 2 kilometres you reach the E7 and Dyranut (P/35).

Route 3: AURLANDSDALEN

The walk from Finse to Aurlandsdalen, located between the Jotunheimen and the Hardangervidda, is one of Norway's classic walks. Years ago, when the only access to either end of the trail was by rail, you'd take the train to Finse to begin your walk and return to Finse via the Flåm line. This limitation ended in the 1970s when a very controversial road was built through the Aurland valley in connection with the development of hydroelectric power. Today buses link Geiterygghytta, Steinbergdalen, Østerbø, Vassbygdi, Aurland and Flåm.

The trail through the Aurlandsdalen valley, starting at Hol via Geiterygghytta and extending all the way down the valley to Aurland, traces the final miles of an ancient path that connected eastern and western Norway. It was probably used as early as the Viking Age. For hundreds of later years cattle were driven through the valley. Until 1900 there were permanent settlements along Strandavatnet. At Sinjarheim, considered one of the first settlements of the Viking Age, there is evidence of permanent habitation until the 1920s.

In the pre-road years the path followed the river. The trail from Geiterygghytta to Østerbø now runs high above the river, though the road is visible in many places. The most famous part of the trail, between Østerbø and Vassbygdi, has been robbed of some of its wild character and flow in the river has been reduced. Other mountain areas in Norway offer remote walks untouched by civilization. If you wish to get away from it all, try any of the other walks described in this book.

As you depart on foot north from the Finse Railway, you get fine views of the Hardangerjøkulen, one of the largest glaciers in Norway.

Reindeer near Geiterygghytta, Aurlandsdalen

After the railway opened in 1909, it developed into one of Norway's main tourist attractions. During the winter of 1920 three skiers died on the west side of Hardangerjøkulen. The party set out from the Finse Hotel on the way to a small unstaffed hut on the glacier, Demmevasshytta. Weather quickly deteriorated, leading to the death of the three skiers. The tragedy gave momentum to the establishment of the Norwegian Red Cross and the progress of the Norwegian Mountain Touring Association in marking the trails between cabins.

During the war the occupying forces wanted to build a landing strip at Hardangerjøkulen. The first plane to take off crashed after they were unable to build a level area, and final plans for an airport

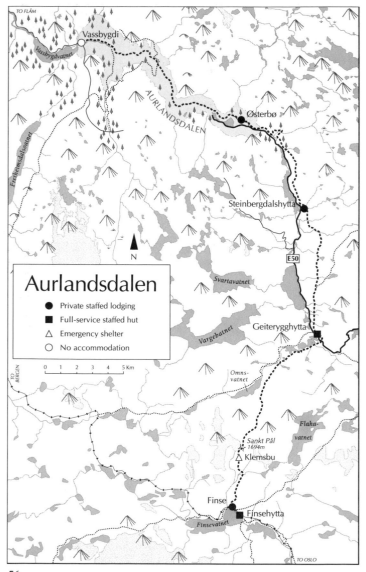

TO FLÅM

Vassbygdi

Vassbygdvatnet

AURLANDSDALEN

Østerbø

Freiheimsdalsvatnet

Steinbergdalshytta

N

E50

Svartavatnet

Aurlandsdalen

● Private staffed lodging

■ Full-service staffed hut

△ Emergency shelter

○ No accommodation

Vargebatnet

Geiterygghytta

TO BERGEN

0 1 2 3 4 5 Km

Omns-vatnet

Flaka-vatnet

Sankt Pål
1694m

△ Klemsbu

Finse

Finsehytta

Finsevatnet

TO OSLO

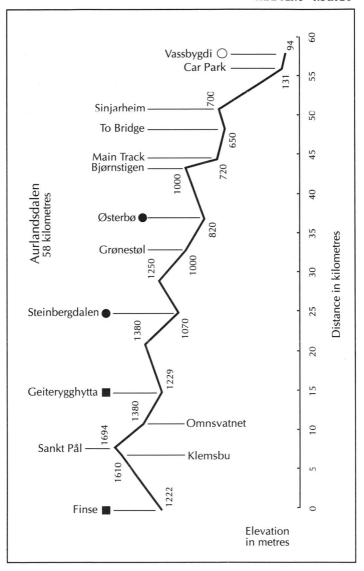

Aurlandsdalen
58 kilometres

Distance in kilometres

Elevation
in metres

Vassbygdi ○ —— 94
Car Park —— 131
Sinjarheim —— 700
To Bridge —— 650
Main Track —— 720
Bjørnstigen —— 1000
Østerbø ● —— 820
Grønestøl —— 1000
1250
Steinbergdalen ● —— 1070
1380
Geiterygghytta ■ —— 1229
1380
Omnsvatnet
Sankt Pål —— 1694
Klemsbu
1610
1222
Finse ■

were never developed.

Since 1958 the Hardangerjøkulen has been one of the centres for DNT's mountaineering courses. Today there is nothing unusual about crossing the Hardangerjøkulen, especially during fine spring weather. On 17 May many people climb to the top of Hardangerjøkulen to celebrate Norway's national holiday.

After completing your walk in Aurlandsdalen you will want to treat yourself to a ride on the Flåm Railway, an extension of the Oslo-Bergen line. The famous side-line to Flåm from Myrdal was proposed in 1923, but not completed until 20 years later. The 20-kilometre long electric rail line has a normal gauge. Its total rise of 864 metres gives it an average elevation of 55%, making it one of the steepest railways in the world. The upper section comprises a series of hairpin turns, many inside the mountain. Twenty tunnels make up 28% of the railway's length. The one hour journey boasts of views of breathtaking mountains and scenic waterfalls.

Distance:	58 kilometres
Time:	3-4 days
Rating:	Moderate
Maps:	1416 I Aurlandsdalen, 1416 II Hardangerjøkulen, (1416 IV Aurland)
Start Altitude:	Finse, 1222 metres
Highest Point:	Near Sankt Pål, 1694 metres
Base:	Geilo
Major Access:	Oslo/Bergen

FINSE (1222m) to GEITERYGGHYTTA (1229m) via SANKT PÅL (1694m)
5 hours, 15 kilometres

Elevation:	Moderate, steep
Features:	Train (Finse), store, mountain shelter, bus (Geiterygghytta), permanent snow crossing, glacier views

Finse is Norway's premier cross-country ski area. At Easter time hundreds of people come here to enjoy the splendid scenery, camaraderie, and fine marked winter tracks. DNT's Finsehytta (B/150) affords a splendid location below the glacier Hardangerjøkulen, situated on a peninsula 10 minutes on foot south-east from the railway station.

Directly from the station, begin by walking north across the tracks and locate the Ts on the hillside among the houses ahead of you. Over the next 3 hours your ascent is steady to near Sankt Pål, your high point for the day and a western spur of the large Hallingskarvet ridge. Views to the south, especially of the Hardangerjøkulen, improve as you ascend; you can also see the Hardangervidda plateau. After about $2^{1}/_{2}$ hours you pass Klemsbu, a small shelter, and you are only about 30 minutes from Sankt Pål. Much of this part of the walk will be snow-covered in early season. Route finding presents no difficulty if the weather is good. At the top cross a small glacier where there are no crevasses. Your descent will be steep until you reach the far end of Omnsvatnet and pass a rocky outcropping at about 1400 metres. Then you walk down gradually above the river and tarns and along the lake's western shore to the hut Geiterygghytta (B/82). This is also a popular cross-country ski destination during spring skiing. The bus from Geilo stops south-east down the service road, 20 minutes away on foot.

GEITERYGGHYTTA (1229m) to STEINBERGDALEN (1070m) 3 hours, 13 kilometres

Elevation:	Gradual
Features:	Bus (Geiterygghytta and Steinbergdalen)

Follow the road west of the lodge up the slope of Sundhellerskarvet. Your path is rocky in places, and there may be patches of snow, as you pass under the imposing Sundhellerskarvet. Turn west at the junction at Rossdalen and continue south of Bolhovd to the day's high point at 1250 metres. A moderate descent delivers you to the private lodge at Steinbergdalen (P/50).

You'll be high above the Aurland road, which was built for hydroelectric development in the valley. It remains the only ferry-free road between Oslo and Bergen. Even at your elevation you feel the road far below, and it may be difficult to imagine how wild the scenery was here before the road's controversial construction.

STEINBERGDALEN (1070m) to ØSTERBØ (820m) via HIGH POINT (1250m)
4 hours, 12 kilometres

Elevation:	Gradual
Features:	Bus (Steinbergdalen and Østerbø)

The new path now runs along the hillside above the river valley. From Steinbergdalen follow the Ts north from the lodge on a gradual ascent above the dam. At times you come much closer to the road than you did on the journey from Geiterygghytta. After 1¹/₂ hours you reach the high point of 1250 metres and mountains come into view. From the top, the path stays on an even contour line as you scramble around several rocky outcrops. Snow is usually gone from this area in early season. Finally you reach the water station at Grønestøl. As the trail winds around to head west through the birch trees, you can see a wonderful waterfall from the River Grøna. Continue along the pleasant valley to the two private huts at Østerbø (P/110).

ØSTERBØ (820m) to VASSBYGDI (94m) via BJØRNSTIGEN (1000m)
6 hours, 21 kilometres

Elevation:	Parts extremely steep, moderate, gradual
Features:	Aurlandsdalen valley, bus

For the first hour after you leave Østerbø you follow the valley downstream, walking on the river's true right. You see plunging streams and huge cliffs on the opposite side of the river. At Holmen the route divides, and a low-level easier but less scenic route heads south-west. At the Holmen junction the high-level route continues west and follows the large Ts up a slippery rocky slope. You ascend for 30 minutes past a summer home. This route is indicated on the map M711 as a secondary trail. At Bjørnstigen (1000m) your route turns north and levels out. At a splendid viewpoint, shown on some postcards, you can see all the way to the Aurlandsdalen valley with its steep cliffs. There follows an extremely sharp descent into the valley with cables for protection over the steep and slippery rocks. After 30-45 minutes of knee-wrenching descent you reach the main track again and turn north. Five minutes more brings you to a turnoff west to Little Hell Cave, Vetlahelvete. This detour is worth the short 5 minute walk to the domed water-filled cave. The walls are smooth, and there is a narrow open space at the top which lets in a bit of light.

Back again on the main track, proceed straight ahead from the turnoff. In 10 minutes the main track veers west and begins a slow descent to the river, while a secondary trail continues straight ahead. You now pass under high rock walls with the wild plunging river below. The trail splits with the western branch heading across a footbridge to the river's true left. Continue on the river's true right taking the northern branch at the junction, and in 10 minutes pass a waterfall at Veiverdalen, a nice spot for a break. In 10 more minutes you pass the summer farm at Sinjarheim and turn west. Below the farm your route which was originally blasted out of rock walls, follows the riverside. Eventually you join the trees as you wind your way to the valley's bottom to the car park. Twenty more minutes along the road puts you in the hamlet of Vassbygdi, with its huge power station, and to the bus stop at the kiosk.

ALTERNATIVE ROUTES

The Hardangervidda offers an endless variety of routes. In the west, another classic route requires taking the bus to Haukeliseter and walking north to Hellevassbu and Litlos. Continuing north, you join Route 1 Western Hardangervidda at Torehytta. This takes you right past the base of Hårteigen, an irresistible temptation for scramblers. In the central area you can continue west from Sandhaug to Litlos or east to Lågaros. Rauhellern is joined by multiple tracks: south from Lågaros and north from Heinseter. If early season snow blocks your route from Finse you can join the Aurlandsdalen walk (Route 3) at Geiterygghytta via bus from Geilo. Finally, a route for experienced walkers circles Hardangerjøkulen, but this should be attempted only when the snow has melted from the path.

West Central Mountains

Route 4: JOTUNHEIMEN EAST TO WEST
Route 5: JOTUNHEIMEN SOUTH
Route 6: JOTUNHEIMEN WEST

Where do you find more blue the sky?
Where do more merrily
The brooks run through the meadow
To bathe the many flowers?

The Boys National Anthem, Norway
by Henrik Wergeland

The Jotunheimen, or the Home of the Giants, long known as Norway's premier walking area, lives up to its reputation. Covering only 3900 square kilometres, it offers an amazing concentration of high peaks, more than 200 of them rising above 1900 metres. There are no public roads; all visitors to the area's interior either walk or ski in.

The two famous lakes in the Jotunheimen, Gjende and Bygdin, which UNESCO includes among the most important lakes of the world, are well known in literature (Ibsen, *Peer Gynt*; *Three in Norway by Two of Them*). Glacially fed green Lake Gjende is 18 kilometres long and 146 metres deep. On Lake Gjende boats will transport you to the huts of Gjendebu and Memurubu, and across Lake Bygdin to Fondsbu. Norway's highest waterfall, Vettisfossen, with a 275 metre drop, is located a short walk from the Vetti tourist hut.

In Jotunheimen you will find Norway's and Northern Europe's two highest peaks, Galdhøpiggen (2469m) and Glittertind (2464m). Galdhøpiggen and Glittertind alternate as Norway's highest mountain. Glittertind is actually the highest when the glacier, which covers the top, is included in the measurement. According to the M711 map of 1981 Glittertind is 2472 metres, 3 metres higher than Galdhøpiggen. Repeat measurements in 1984 reduced

Glittertind to 2464 metres, with the height varying from year to year depending on the thickness of its glacier. Galdhøpiggen, free from snow in the summer, was measured at 2469 metres. Both are accessible via trails to the fit walker.

Three outstanding routes are described here. This first is a classic tour (Route 4 Jotunheimen East to West) which crosses the park near its northern high peaks. Beginning at Gjendesheim this route loops north to Spiterstulen and ends in the west at Vetti. Ascents of Norway's two highest peaks are possible on trails and guided groups cross the glaciers to the top of Galdhøpiggen. The second tour crosses the southern part of the Jotunheimen (Route 5 Jotunheimen South) and is highlighted by a visit to Lake Gjende and to Fannaråkhytta, Norway's highest mountain hut. If your time is limited few tours beat this 3-4 day western Jotunheimen ramble (Route 6 Jotunheimen West) which also includes Fannaråkhytta and visits one of my favourite huts, Skogadalsbøen.

The climate in the Jotunheimen varies noticeably. Cloud and drizzle, especially common in the western fjord area around Fannaråkhytta and Vetti, can extend easterly to Skogadalsbøen. On the other hand Spiterstulen and other more easterly locations such as Gjendesheim boast drier and sunnier conditions, thus increasing your chances of a successful ascent of Galdhøpiggen and Glittertind.

TRANSPORT

From the eastern side of the park off road 51, Gjendesheim is served several times a day by bus from Otta and Fagernes. You can reach Otta by train from Oslo or Trondheim, and Fagernes by bus from Oslo. In the summer a boat service across Lake Gjende links Gjendesheim with Memurubu and Gjendebu. If you wish to free yourself of the burden of your rucksack you can have it sent ahead on the boat.

If you are joining your tour from the western fjords or from Bergen you can take the famous mountain railway to Flåm, ferry to Årdalstangen, and bus to Øvre Årdal and Hjelle. A 1¹/₂ hour walk up the road brings you to your first night at the old farm Vetti. Though this sounds complicated, the efficiency of the Norwegian transport system obviates difficulty. Turtagrø, Sognefjellhytta and Krossbu are located on road 55, a splendid road through this mountain country. Daily summer buses from the train station at Otta go to Lom, Sognefjellhytta, Krossbu, Turtagrø and Øvre Årdal.

Route 4: JOTUNHEIMEN EAST TO WEST

Distance:	101 kilometres
Time:	7 days
Rating:	Strenuous
Maps:	1517 I Tyin, 1517 IV Hurrungane, 1518 II Galdhøpiggen 1518 III Sygnefjell, 1617 IV Gjende, 1618 III Glittertinden
	Jotunheimen 1:100 000
Start Altitude:	Gjendesheim, 995 metres
Highest Point:	Glittertind, 2464 metres
Base:	Otta/Fagernes
Major Access:	Oslo/Trondheim/Bergen

GJENDESHEIM (995m) to MEMURUBU (1008m) via BESSEGGEN RIDGE (1743m)
6 hours, 15 kilometres

Elevation:	Parts extremely steep, parts moderate
Features:	Besseggen ridge, boat service, luggage transport, bus (Gjendesheim)

Over centuries of mountain walking in Norway many a tour has begun at Gjendesheim, on the eastern end of Lake Gjende. Three of the huts used in these walks, Gjendesheim, Memurubu and Gjendebu, were built in the 1870s. At Gjendesheim the original hut, built in 1878, is located on the south side of the river, accessible by rowboat. Looking across Lake Gjende from Gjendesheim makes for a popular photograph, with many a wild and rarely visited peak in view on the south side of the lake. On the north side steep rock walls rise. The first break in this fortress occurs at Memurubu, the private

---

Above Memurubu, Jotunheimen

lodge reached on foot at the end of the first day of this tour.

To begin your walk climb steeply from DNT's Gjendesheim (B/143) about one kilometre on the same trail that heads north to Glitterheim. In 30 minutes turn west towards Besseggen, pass through the Veltløyfti gorge, and continue for 2 hours upwards to the wide top of Veslfjellet (1743m). Your climb finally levels out and if you are lucky you will see reindeer here. Next start your descent on the famous Besseggen ridge, which runs between Lake Gjende (984m) and Lake Bessvatn (1373m). Though the ridge does narrow to about 50 metres wide in spots, it is easy to avoid walking too close to the 400 metre drop-off straight down into Lake Gjende. In a spot or two it is narrow enough to view down into both sides, and several places require scrambling. If you suffer from extreme fear of heights or dizziness, you may prefer to forgo this route. The dangers of this ridge are often exaggerated, but the much vaunted views live up to their reputation.

Your tour along the Besseggen ridge is one of Norway's most famous walks. In Ibsen's play *Peer Gynt* Peer rides an ox wildly along this renowned ridge. Over 30,000 people walk the Besseggen ridge during the summer months. Due to the crowds, Norwegians have renamed it Karl Johans Way, after the main street in Oslo. *Three in Norway by Two of Them* published in English in 1882 humorously chronicles the visit of three British tourists to the Jotunheimen.

You will soon notice the contrast between the green colour of Gjende and blue Bessvatn. The source of the green of Gjende is the glaciers from the upper mountains which send clay particles down the rivers to the lake. Bessvatnet, on the other hand, not a glacial lake, is blue.

Three hours from the start you reach the south end of Bessvatn as the path ascends moderately to a small lake below the peak Besshø and crosses a plateau. You begin your final winding descent to the new lodge at Memurubu (P/140) about 20 minutes past tomorrow's turnoff to Glitterheim. Many huts in the Jotunheimen, such as Memurubu, are privately run, and their prices are higher than at DNT lodges.

If you have good weather I recommend spending an extra day

Summit of Galdhøpiggen, Norway's highest peak, 2469 metres, Jotunheimen

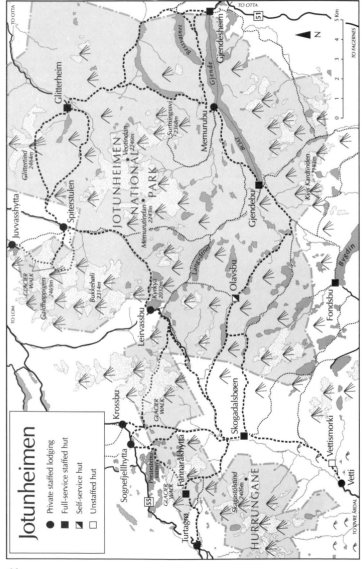

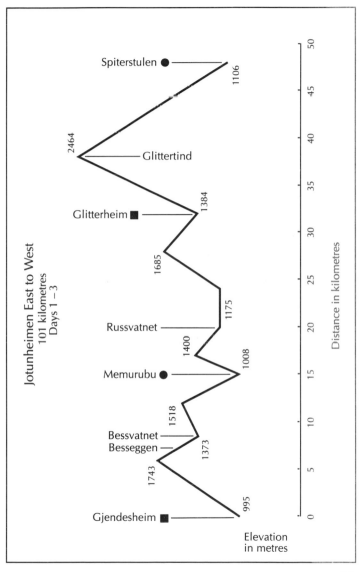

Jotunheimen East to West
101 kilometres
Days 1 – 3

Spiterstulen ●
1106
2464
Glittertind
1384
Glitterheim ■
1685
1175
Russvatnet
1400
1008
Memurubu ●
1518
Bessvatnet
Besseggen
1373
1743
995
Gjendesheim ■

Elevation
in metres

Distance in kilometres

at Memurubu, and walking to Gjendebu (Route 5 Jotunheimen South). Use the boat to bring you back to Memurubu in the evening.

MEMURUBU (1008m) to GLITTERHEIM (1384m) via RUSSVATNET (1175m) and HIGH POINT (1685m)
6 hours, 17 kilometres

Elevation:	Steep, parts moderate, parts almost level
Features:	Waterfall, short snow sections

From Memurubu backtrack steeply from yesterday's climb to the turnoff to Glitterheim. Turn north at the trail junction, and in 15 minutes pass into Russglopet gorge, which may be snow-covered, and walk another 45 minutes moderately downhill to the south edge of Russvatnet. For $1^{1/2}$ hours or more you wander along the western shore of the lake, passing a marvellous waterfall. Some 20 minutes past Sundodden point, and about halfway along the lake shore, you begin a steady rise north. Cross the footbridge and continue to ascend to the snow fields of Hestlœgerhöi, just below the high point on the ridge. Following the river you can see Glitterheim (B/130), your destination for the night, still $1^{1/2}$ hours away.

GLITTERHEIM (1384m) to SPITERSTULEN (1106m) via GLITTERTIND (2464m) (High Route)
7 hours, 16 kilometres

Elevation:	Extremely steep, parts steep
Features:	Mountain views, Norway's second highest peak, snow sections, bus (Spiterstulen)

A rewarding day awaits you. From Glitterheim take the trail about $1/2$ kilometre west toward Steinbudalen. Here the trail turns north and you begin a long, slow and steady ascent up the southern slope of Glittertinden. The ascent of 1000-plus metres requires some $3^{1/2}$ hours. If the visibility is low or the winds high use great caution. Glittertind was once thought to be higher than Galdhøpiggen, and in some years with heavy snow cover its top may just be a metre or so higher than its better known neighbour.

The route leads west across the summit snowfield. Take care not

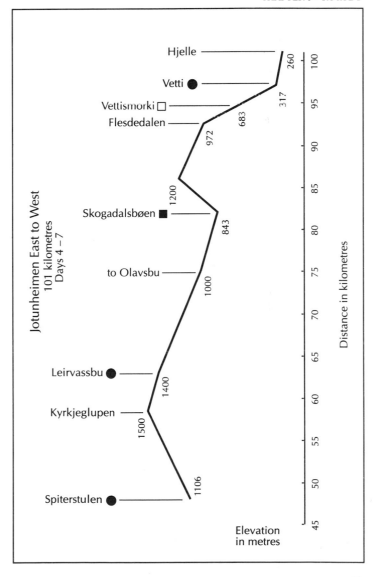

Jotunheimen East to West
101 kilometres
Days 4 – 7

Hjelle

Vetti ●

Vettismorki □

Flesdedalen

Skogadalsbøen ■

to Olavsbu

Leirvassbu ●

Kyrkjeglupen

Spiterstulen ●

260

317

683

972

1200

843

1000

1400

1500

1106

Distance in kilometres

100 95 90 85 80 75 70 65 60 55 50 45

Elevation
in metres

to walk too close to the northern precipice. Once you are on the top the cairns lead you down steeply to flatter terrain where you join the lower route from Glitterheim to Spiterstulen. The low route is described next.

GLITTERHEIM (1384m) to SPITERSTULEN (1106m) via VESLGLUPEN (1660m) (Low Route)
5 hours, 16 kilometres

Elevation: Moderate, parts extremely steep, parts almost level
Features: Mountain views, snow sections, bus (Spiterstulen)

This is an easier route than the high route over Glittertinden described above. From the hut take the track south across the river and continue south-west below Ryggehøi, north of the River Veo. After about 5 kilometres and $1^1/2$ hours the trail turns north and passes through the Veslglupen gorge. There is a short steep ascent for 30-45 minutes over talus and across snow in early season. Tarns dot the day's high point as you cross to the flat plateau Stautflyi. To the south there are fine views to the high peaks of Veotindan (2240m), the Veobreen glacier and Memurutinden peaks. After about $3^1/2$ hours you pass the turnoff to the top of Glittertinden. Crossing the flats you get your first view of Galdhøpiggen, Norway's highest peak, and begin a steep descent to Spiterstulen (P/120/ cafeteria/road access/bus/glacier tours). Upon reaching the road turn west and walk one kilometre to the lodge.

It is thought that the original house at Spiterstulen dates from 1790. Visitors seem to have come to the area for centuries before that to hunt and to pasture reindeer and cows. Today it is a busy tourist centre. Many walkers pass through; some arrive only for the daily guided ascents of Galdhøpiggen or tours of the icefalls. In high summer Spiterstulen is always full, and overflow walkers are housed in two crowded dormitories next to the main lodge. If you want a private room it is essential to call ahead for a reservation. If you want full board and plan to eat in the dining room, rather than using the less costly cafeteria, your request is more likely to be honoured.

There are daily guided glacier walks to the top of Galdhøpiggen. Walkers supplied with instep crampons are roped together in long

*Glacier walk to top of Galdhøpiggen, Norway's highest peak,
2469 metres, Jotunheimen*

71

lines as they weave in and out of the seracs near the terminus of the glacier and then cross the main glacier. Unroping at the far end of the glacier, there is an extremely steep 45 minute rocky ascent with scrambling. You come out on the main trail about 20 minutes below the summit. On a fine day the summit can be crowded; most walkers arrive on the trail from Spiterstulen. The kiosk sells T-shirts, commemorative pins, and hot drinks. The hut is supplied by helicopter and the warden lives there for several weeks in the summer. Views of the entire Jotunheimen range are splendid.

You can also sneak up on Galdhøpiggen from the other side from Juvvasshytta (P/75), where there is summer skiing. Daily guided glacier walks leave this hut in the summertime. Since Juvvasshytta is located at 1800 metres your climb is much less than if you start from Spiterstulen (1106m). There is daily bus service to Juvvasshytta from Otta via Lom.

SPITERSTULEN (1106m) to LEIRVASSBU (1400m) via KYRKJEGLUPEN (1500m)
5 hours, 15 kilometres

Elevation: Moderate

From Spiterstulen, you walk a gradual rise up the Visdalen valley, remaining on the eastern shore of the river, leaving the high peaks behind. After 2 hours pass a turnoff south to Gjendebu. Our trail gradually turns west and continues to rise up to the Kvrkjeglupen gap (1500m). The majestic Church Steeple, Kyrkja, rising symmetrically to the south, can be climbed most easily from Leirvassbu. Crossing through the gap you pass close to several icy tarns and cross along the north side of the lake to reach Leirvassbu (P/120/glacier guide over Smørstabbreen). During the summer there are glacier walks over Smørstabbreen to Krossbu/ Sognefjellhytta. This is a marvellous way to extend this tour. Using glacier guides, one day cross the glacier to Sognefjellhytta and the next day cross Fannaråkbreen to Fannaråkhytta. The next day's walk brings you down to Skogadalsbøen. This route is described in the opposite direction under Route 6 Jotunheimen West.

Below Kyrkja near Leirvassbu, Jotunheimen

LEIRVASSBU (1400m) to SKOGADALSBØEN (843m)
5 hours 30 minutes, 19 kilometres

Elevation: Moderate
Features: Waterfalls

A slow gradual descent marks most of the day. From Leirvassbu follow the vehicle road south-west along a chain of lakes for $2^{1}/_{2}$

73

kilometres until you reach a trail branch to the Smørstabbreen glacier. The road and trail here can be covered with snow well into August. Take the left-hand branch south-west and continue to follow the road down the Gravdlaen valley. After 7 kilometres you come to another large lake, dammed at the far end. Though the trail is rocky it is not difficult. After $3^{1/2}$ hours you come to the turnoff to Olavsbu, still 12 kilometres east up the valley. Ninety minutes later you reach the turnoff west to Fannaråkhytta and Turtagrø. A $^{1/2}$ hour walk south through the birch trees gets you to Skogadalsbøen (B/55), guarded by a large black Newfoundland dog. In a splendid setting nestled among surrounding peaks, it is one of my favourite DNT huts. The proprietors speak fluent English, and are full of excellent suggestions for day walks. Let them direct you to Vormeli or guide you on a climb up one of the neighbouring peaks or visit Fannaråkhytta. Be sure to sample some of their home-made brew.

SKOGADALSBØEN (843m) to VETTI (317m) via HIGH POINT (1200m)
5 hours, 15 kilometres

Elevation:	Moderate, parts extremely steep
Features:	Mountain views, waterfalls, Norway's highest waterfall, Vettisfossen

This is a spectacular walk. From the hut, head south up the small hill and cross the footbridge a few minutes from the hut. For the first $1^{1/2}$ hours you make a gradual ascent to reach the day's high point below Mount Friken (1503m). During the first part of the day you get views to the west of the Hurrungane range and glaciers. Hope for fine weather to gain the best view of these spectacular peaks, glaciers and valleys. Now follow a gradual downhill to a farm at Flesdedalen, followed by more downhill on wet ground to Vettismorki (U/4), where there are numerous summer cabins. Thirty minutes from the cabins you cross a footbridge over a raging river, and there are splendid views down into the valley. A steep 400 metre descent to the old farm Vetti (P/21) follows. A 20 minute detour from Vetti takes you to Vettisfossen, Norway's highest waterfall, with a vertical drop of 275 metres.

VETTI (317m) TO HJELLE (260m)
1 hour 15 minutes, 4 kilometres

Elevation:	Gradual
Features:	Road, bus/taxi option (Hjelle)

From Vetti head downhill on the paved road south for one hour to Hjelle, where there is a small souvenir stand. Bus or taxi service links you to Øvre Årdal (H/bus/taxi/ferry connections/limited supplies) or you can walk the 8 kilometres into town. Bus service links you to Årdalstangen with ferry connections to Bergen, or you can take a bus to Fagernes with connections to Oslo.

Route 5: JOTUNHEIMEN SOUTH

This highly recommended tour crosses through the southern Jotunheimen from east to west. If you have only a few days to spare, this is the trip I recommend. Though it does not include the high peak area to the north (Route 4), it is just as scenic, uses friendlier DNT huts and is less crowded during the high season.

Your first 2 days, very typical of Norwegian mountain walking, traverse the high ridges to the north of Lake Gjende. You pass through a valley between two high mountain ridges, and visit the self-service hut of Olavsbu as well as the full-service friendly hut of Skogadalsbøen. Your reward at the end is Norway's highest mountain hut at Fannaråkhytta, a sight not to be missed. If you are lucky enough to have a fortnight at your disposal, the grand circle of the Jotunheimen, combining Tours 4 and 5, is one of Europe's classic mountain tours. This trip includes climbs of the two highest peaks in Norway and two guided glacier crossings.

Distance:	78.5 kilometres
Time:	4-6 days
Rating:	Strenuous
Maps:	1517 I Tyin, 1517 IV Hurrungane, 1518 III Sygnefjell, 1617 IV Gjende, 1618 III Glittertinden Jotunheimen 1:100 000

Start Altitude:	Gjendesheim, 995 metres
Highest Point:	Fannaråkhytta, 2068 metres
Base:	Fagernes/Otta
Major Access:	Oslo/Trondheim

GJENDESHEIM (995m) to MEMURUBU (1008m) via BESSEGGEN
6 hours, 15 kilometres

Elevation:	Parts extremely steep, moderate
Features:	Besseggen ridge, boat option, luggage transport

This day is described under Route 4 Jotunheimen East to West.

MEMURUBU (1008m) to GJENDEBU (990m) via GRUNNEVATNET (1443m) and BUKKELAGERET
5 hours 15 minutes, 11 kilometres

Elevation:	Steep, parts extremely steep
Features:	Boat option, luggage transport

Many consider this one of the more impressive walks in the area. Unfortunately, it's often missed. Along with fine lake views you'll see many of the peaks and glaciers of the Jotunheimen. Our route crosses to the true right of the river above the Memurudal valley and follows the path through the steep gorge up the ridge west of the hut. You'll climb a series of ledges and get your first glimpse of the many peaks in the distance. To the south you'll catch sight of Høgebrotet, Tjørnholstind and Leirungstind. Looking back to the east you'll see yesterday's route over the Besseggen ridge and Besshø. In the north you'll view the Memurubu glacier and the peaks of Semmeltind and Stordalshø.

After reaching the top of the ridge you skirt some mountain lakes and pass the trail which marks the lower route to Memurubu. Continue downward and in 2 kilometres pass another turnoff west to Leirvassbu. A railing aids you for your one hour steep descent down Bukkelœgret. After reaching Lake Gjende you need another 30 minutes along the shore to get to DNT's Gjendebu (B/115).

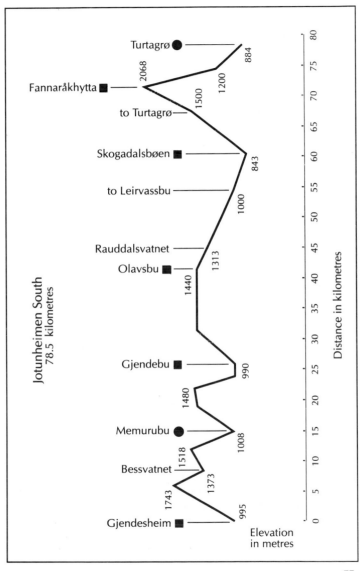

Jotunheimen South
78.5 kilometres

Turtagrø ● 884
2068
1200
Fannaråkhytta ■ 1500
to Turtagrø
Skogadalsbøen ■ 843
to Leirvassbu 1000
Rauddalsvatnet 1313
Olavsbu ■ 1440
Gjendebu ■ 990
1480
Memurubu ● 1008
1518
Bessvatnet 1373
1743
Gjendesheim ■ 995

Distance in kilometres

Elevation
in metres

77

GJENDEBU (990m) to OLAVSBU (1440m)
5 hours, 15.5 kilometres

Elevation: Gradual, almost level

From Gjendebu take the trail heading south towards Fondsbu and
Eidsbugarden. You'll ascend very gradually for 2 hours to the
turnoff to Olavsbu. Fine views of Gjende lie behind you. If the
weather is good an alternative route ascends Gjendestunga (1516m)
behind the hut, and from the summit follows the ridge lines south
until it meets the trail. Upon reaching the turnoff to Olavsbu head
west, as the main path continues southward to Eidsbugarden. You
ramble along now for about 3 hours with little elevation change.
Passing several lovely lakes you proceed through the Rauddalen
valley in pleasant quiet surroundings. Snow may cover this area
into late July, so be careful not to walk too close to the water's edge.
Finally you reach the comfortable self-service hut at Olavsbu (SS/
35).

Self-service hut Olavsbu, Jotunheimen

OLAVSBU (1440m) to SKOGADALSBØEN (843m)
6 hours, 19 kilometres

Elevation:	Almost level, moderate
Features:	Mountain views

This is another pleasant day of valley walking. Your route from Olavsbu heads east and in 45 minutes passes along the east end of the large Rauddalsvatnet. At the lake's western end you meet a turnoff south to a higher route to Skogadalsbøen; this may be snow-covered and very wet well into July. Continue down the valley on the river's true left passing a chain of lakes. In one hour you drop steeply south-west down the valley, passing the turnoff to Leirvassbu. Head down the wide open valley until you reach the birch trees and a new river valley. Turning south, the trail to Krossbu joins you from the north. In 20 minutes you pass the turnoff to Fannaråkhytta, tomorrow's destination. A 30 minute easy stroll brings you to Skogadalsbøen (B/55) (see under Route 4).

SKOGADALSBØEN (843m) to FANNARÅKHYTTA (2068m) via
KEISARPASSET (1452m)
4 hours 20 minutes, 11 kilometres

Elevation:	Extremely steep, moderate
Features:	Norway's highest mountain hut, Jotunheimen views

From Skogadalsbøen retrace yesterday's steps for 20 minutes to the turnoff to Turtagrø; the northern branch of the trail continues onto Krossbu. Turn west and cross the River Utla on the bridge. Your route ascends moderately up a lovely valley on the true left of the raging Jervvasselvi. There are splendid views of the Jervvassbu glacier, Gjertvasstind and Skagastölstindane. In 90 minutes you come to the pleasant Jervatnet with a summer cabin on the near end. Cross the outlet to the lake's west side and continue northward on a steep and rocky 100 metre ascent to Keisarpasset, where there is a short cut to Turtagrø. Here you may meet the seemingly ever-present fog. The winter route to Fannaråkhytta has been discontinued due to avalanche danger; you will notice the old trail markers. Cross above the two lakes near the pass and begin your very steep zig-zag ascent to the summit ridge at Fannaråknosi. Once on the ridge it's a mere 20 minutes across the level ridge to Fannaråkhytta (B/35).

In 1926 the Norwegian Tourist Association, in co-operation with the Meteorology Institute, built the cabin at Fannaråken, which at 2068 metres became the country's highest tourist lodge. In 1981 the DNT took over full management of this splendid hut famous for both its views and fog. On some maps this full-service hut is incorrectly listed as a self-service lodge. The staff here works 3-week shifts in the summer, and the supplies arrive by helicopter. Not surprisingly, the menu is limited. If you are lucky you'll be able to see the entire Hurrungane range and most of the Jotunheimen. If not, plan another trip.

You can cross Fannaråkbreen to Sognefjellhytta or Krossbu with a glacier guide during the summer. I recommend that you conclude this tour with this trip described under Route 6 Jotunheimen West.

FANNARÅKHYTTA (2068m) to TURTAGRØ (884m)
3 hours, 7 kilometres

Elevation:	Extremely steep, moderate
Features:	Norway's highest mountain hut, bus (Turtagrø)

If you don't want to take the guided glacier tour, you should exit this way. From the hut head south-west on the rocky trail looking closely for the Ts. Finding the trail will be difficult in the fog; look carefully and do not leave the first marker until you see the next one. The path descends steeply over talus. Levelling out when you reach the river, you continue on the river's true left down the broad river valley. Head west along the road to Turtagrø (P/80). Much of Norway's climbing centres around the town of Turtagrø. Western Norway's most famous climbs include the nearby Skagastølstind (2403m).

Route 6: JOTUNHEIMEN WEST

This is one of my favourite tours in Norway. The 4-day route crosses two glaciers and offers splendid views of some of the high peaks of this famous area. If you have only 3 days at your disposal you can start this tour at Sognefjellhytta and circle between Skogadalsbøen

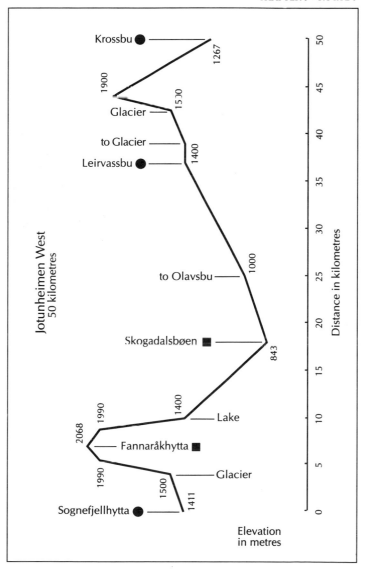

Jotunheimen West
50 kilometres

Krossbu ● ————— 1267
1900
Glacier ——— 1530
to Glacier ——— 1400
Leirvassbu ● ————
1000
to Olavsbu ———
Skogadalsbøen ■ ————— 843
1990 2068
1400
——— Lake
Fannaråkhytta ■ ———
1990 1500
——— Glacier
Sognefjellhytta ● ——— 1411

Distance in kilometres

Elevation
in metres

81

View to Fannaråknosi, Jotunheimen

and Fannaråkhytta. The weather should dictate the direction of your tour; save the glacier crossing for a fine day. If you have another day at your disposal my description also includes a crossing of the Smørstabbreen. Both glacier crossings may be made during the summer with glacier guides.

Distance:	50 kilometres
Time:	3-4 days
Rating:	Strenuous
Maps:	1517 IV Hurrungane, 1518 II Galdhøpiggen, 1518 III Sygnefjell Jotunheimen 1:100 000
Start Altitude:	Sognefjellhytta, 1411 metres
Highest Point:	Fannaråkhytta, 2068 metres
Base:	Otta
Major Access:	Oslo/Trondheim

SOGNEFJELLHYTTA (1411m) to FANNARÅKHYTTA (2068m)
5 hours, 13 kilometres

Elevation:	Moderate, parts steep
Features:	Glacier crossing, mountain views, bus (Sognefjellhytta)

From Sognefjellhytta, a private hut on road 55, follow the cairns south across the rocky landscape for 2 hours to the edge of the Fannaråkbreen glacier. Before you leave check at the lodge for specific information on meeting your guide. During July and August a group is usually led down from Fannaråkhytta in the morning, and back up again in the afternoon. You will need no special equipment. Unless you are trained and experienced in glacier crossings, and are properly equipped, you should cross with a guide. The route circles the eastern edge of the glacier, ascending gradually, but becomes steep just before Fannaråknosi, the rock outcropping of the summit ridge. The last $1^{1/2}$ kilometres heads on a rocky trail directly east to the Fannaråkhytta (B/35), DNT's and Norway's highest mountain hut, with its never-to-be forgotten views. An eerie atmosphere pervades from the heights as mist swirls about and distant mountain peaks loom through its openings.

FANNARÅKHYTTA (2069m) to SKOGADALSBØEN (843m)
3 hours 30 minutes, 11 kilometres

This route is described walking in the opposite direction under Route 5 Jotunheimen South.

SKOGADALSBØEN (843m) to LEIRVASSBU (1400m)
6 hours, 19 kilometres

Today's route is described in the opposite direction under Route 4 Jotunheimen East to West.

LEIRVASSBU (1400m) to KROSSBU (1230m)
6 hours, 15.5 kilometres

Elevation:	Steep, parts moderate
Features:	Glacier crossing, bus (Krossbu)

From the private hut at Leirvassbu your guide will take you all the way to Krossbu. Following the service road south to the edge of Lake 1395, you then head east up the Gravdalspallen to reach the glacier in about one hour. Your first 2 hours on the glacier will take you up a moderately steep ascent for a lunch stop under the Storebjørn summit. Here you will pass the group coming from the other direction. The afternoon is spent slowly descending a moderate slope skirting crevasses and areas of blue ice. The tour will take you most directly to the private hut at Krossbu (P/75) where you can catch a bus home or spend the night.

CHAPTER 7:
North Central Mountains

Route 7: RONDANE TRAVERSE
Route 8: RONDANE TOPS (High Route)
Route 9: RONDANE CIRCLE (Low Route)
Route 10: ALVDAL VESTFJELL (Low Route)
Route 11: ALVDAL VESTFJELL (High Route)

Defiant mountains beckon me
To glory and dream in their Paradise.

Walter A. Starr, Jr.

The Rondane, established in 1962 as Norway's first National Park and now one of the country's most popular walking areas, is located south of the Dovre, east of the Jotunheimen and west of the Østerdalen. The Rondane's 580 square kilometres, one-third in the high alpine zone, appeal to walkers of all ages and abilities. Ten peaks exceed the magical 2000 metre mark; many are accessible to any reasonably fit and eager walker. In the east the gentle Alvdal Vestfjell appeals to older walkers and families with small children.

Wild mountain peaks divide the Rondane into three distinct areas. To the west of the centrally located lake, Rondvatnet, the wild cirques and jagged peaks of Storsmeden (2017m), Sagtinden (2018m) and Veslesmeden (2015m) create an impressive picture. East of the lake tower Rondslottet (2178m), Vinjeronden (2044m) and Storronden (2138m). At the southern end of Rondvatnet, Rondvassbu, the area's main DNT hut, may be conveniently used as a base for the avid peak climber. Further east Høgronden (2114m), linking the lodges of Bjørnhollia and Dørålseter, dominates.

In the east the Alvdal Vestfjell, characterized by summer farms, rolling hills and gentle ascents, offers a climb of Sølnkletten (1827m) with its commanding views of the entire Rondane range. Fewer people visit this area when compared with its neighbour the Rondane. If you are with small children or just not up to a more taxing holiday, it is a wonderful alternative. Routes in the Alvdal

85

Vestfjell can easily be linked with walks in the Rondane by heading west to Straumbu and onto Bjørnhollia. From here you can link up with Rondane Routes 7, 8, and 9.

TRANSPORT
Reaching the Rondane is easy. All starting points for these walks are within an easy day's journey from Oslo or Trondheim. From Otta on the Oslo-Trondheim train route (Dovre Line) buses or taxis connect to the parking area at Spranghaugen through Mysusæter. Rondvassbu is only an hour's walk from the car park. For Route 7 Rondane Traverse the train stop at Hjerkinn is just north of Otta on the Oslo-Trondheim train (Dovre Line). A limited summer bus service links Straumbu with Ringebu. Disembark at Alvdal from the Oslo-Trondheim train (Røros Line) for the Alvdal Vestfjell. A taxi service from Alvdal will take you into the Alvdal Vestfjell.

Familiar DNT trail marker, Rondane

Route 7: RONDANE TRAVERSE
HJERKINN to STRAUMBU

Distance:	64 kilometres
Time:	5-6 days
Rating:	Moderate
Maps:	1519 III Hjerkinn, 1718 I Rondane, 1818 IV Atnsjøen Rondane 1:100 000
Start Altitude:	Hjerkinn, 950 metres
Highest Point:	High point between Hageseter and Grimsdalshytta, 1340 metres
Base:	Otta
Major Access:	Oslo/Trondheim

The proposed 5-6 day crossing of the Rondane range begins from the railway station at Hjerkinn and ends at Straumbu. Your moderate tour can be continued into the Alvdal Vestfjell, or shortened by entering or leaving from Rondvassbu. An extra day or two at Rondvassbu or Bjørnhollia allows time to climb peaks in the area, although these additions will make your day a strenuous one.

HJERKINN (950m) to GRIMSDALSHYTTA (994m) via HAGESETER (916m) and HIGH POINT (1340m)
4 hours 30 minutes, 16 kilometres

Elevation:	Moderate, parts steep
Features:	Railway station (Hjerkinn)

After stepping down from the train at Hjerkinn look for the DNT trail markers just south of the station, below the knoll. If you can't find the trail take the paved road a few minutes into town where you'll see the hotel, campsite and a small store. About 3 minutes before you reach the store, you will see the red T markers heading south into the woods. The trail passes through the woods, paralleling the railway, with good views towards the lake and dam. In 30 minutes you cross the road E6, and after another 15 minutes you pass over the River Folla on a footbridge. You will see Hageseter

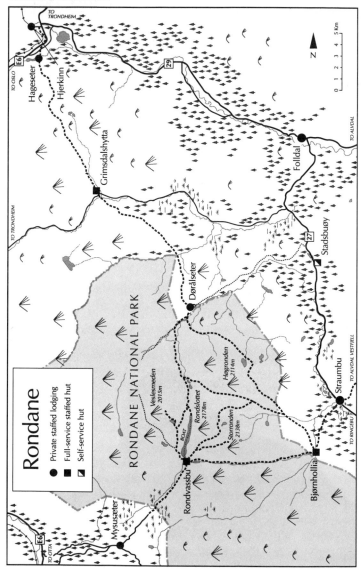

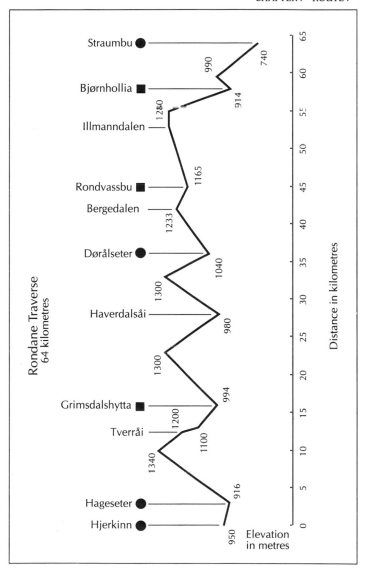

(P/70) a few hundred metres down the road on the left, offering camping and other accommodation for late arrivals.

From the bridge follow the trail markers south up the hill on the true left of the river. After one hour you will cross to the river's true right or eastern shore, gradually gaining elevation. Good views back to town and to the Dovre mountains await you. Shortly at a boggy area, your climb levels out and you pass Stenbuhøi (1354m), the black peak to the east. Two hours from Hageseter you reach the day's high point at 1340 metres, as the views of town are lost from behind. Next for an hour your route follows a slow, gradual, and lovely descent towards the River Tverråi. Just before the river the descent steepens. Proceed cautiously until you reach the footbridge at the bottom. As you leave the river behind you make a short, steep, 15 minute ascent, and finally sight the hut. At the delightful Grimsdalshytta (B/34), several wooden trolls guard the front entrance.

GRIMSDALSHYTTA (994m) to DØRÅLSETER (1040m) via HAVERDALSÅI (980m) via HIGH POINTS (1300m) (above Dørålseter and above Grimsdalshytta)
5 hours 45 minutes, 20 kilometres

Elevation: Gradual, parts steep

From Grimsdalshytta, cross the bridge over the River Grimsi and begin your gradual ascent in trees up the west side of Gravhø. Two hours brings you to a high point (1300m) with good views back to the valley. A steep descent into Haverdalsåi valley will test your knees. Turn west if heading upvalley to Haverdalssetra (P/40). If not, a few minutes' walk east and downstream will take you to the bridge across the river. A steep, rocky ascent on talus follows and after 30 minutes the trail narrows into a rocky passageway. This area may be snow-covered well into the summer. It takes about 2 hours to reach the top at the notch; a 45 minute steep descent to upper Dørålseter (P/100) follows. The middle private hut is so well known for its good cooking that you need a reservation in high season.

DØRÅLSETER (1040m) to RONDVASSBU (1165m) via RONDVATNET (1165m)
3 hours, 9 kilometres

Elevation: Almost level
Features: Summer boat service, peak climb (optional)

From the huts head south-west up the Dørålen valley and after one kilometre cross to the river's true right. Follow the river for another kilometre, passing the turnoff to Høgronden. Cross over the Bergedalen and after one kilometre turn south and follow the path above the river. In about an hour you will reach a series of lakes, where a turn east will take you up the Langglupdalen to Bjørnhollia. Continue south following a gradual ascent to Rondvatnet. Here about 3 hours from Dørålseter, you can pick up a boat (July and August only) to Rondvassbu (B/128). Just before the lake another trail turns steeply up the slopes of Veslesmeden, and 2 hours walking high above Rondvatnet will bring you to Rondvassbu as well. If you wish to climb Veslesmeden you will need another 4 hours. This route is described under Route 8 Rondane Tops.

RONDVASSBU (1165m) to BJØRNHOLLIA (914m) via ILLMANNDALEN (1280m)
4 hours, 13 kilometres

Terrain: Moderate, parts almost level

Unless you are a peak climber and choose the high route to Bjørnhollia, another easy day follows. From outside the front door of Rondvassbu take the extremely steep slope east and after 10 minutes branch east again, when the main trail veers north to Storronden. An easy traverse along the Illmanndalen awaits you and in the ensuing hour you pass several pleasant mountain lakes. After $2^{1}/_{2}$ hours you reach the divide at 1300 metres, the day's high point. Now you begin your descent along the north edge of Illmanndalen to Bjørnhollia (B/90). This is one of my favourite huts in the Rondane, and it is a fine spot for a rest day. Day options include a trip to Villmannsdalen, or for the hearty, a climb of Rondslottet or Høgronden (see under Route 8 Rondane Tops). Several of the hills around the hut offer views of the surrounding

Bjørnhollia, Rondane

valleys. Here you can join Lillehammer-Rondane trail and head south to the self-service hut Eldåbu. Several days' walking further south from Eldåbu brings you to Lillehammer, the site of the 1994 Winter Olympics.

BJØRNHOLLIA (914m) to STRAUMBU (740m) via HIGH POINT (990m)
2 hours, 6 kilometres

Elevation:	Almost level, parts steep
Features:	Bus (Straumbu) (limited service)

Today's pleasant walk begins with a steep 100-metre ascent up the hill to the east of Bjørnhollia. After 45 minutes you'll descend gradually to a marshy area where you'll have outstanding views of the Rondane peaks of Rondslottet and Høgronden, shrouded in snow until the middle of summer. Continuing across the flats you'll descend steeply for 50 metres, pass through the trees for around 15 minutes and reach Straumbu (P/30), across the bridge on the other side of the road. This is a good entrance point into the neighbouring

Alvdal Vestfjell. From here buses run on limited summer timetable to Ringebu and on to Oslo.

Route 8: RONDANE TOPS
RONDVASSBU to RONDVASSBU
(High Route)

Distance:	60 kilometres
Time:	3 days
Rating:	Strenuous
Maps:	Rondane 1718 I, Atnsjøen 1818 IV Rondane 1:100 000
Start Altitude:	Rondvassbu, 1165 metres
Highest Point:	Rondslottet, 2178 metres
Base:	Otta
Major Access:	Oslo/Trondheim

This 3-day circuit ascends three wonderful peaks in the Rondane: Rondslottet, Høgronden and Veslesmeden. Only if you are comfortable with long days on rocky terrain should you attempt the full circuit. Those who do tackle it are rewarded with marvellous summit views, and visits to the splendid DNT huts at Rondvassbu and Bjørnhollia.

If you consider the route below too difficult for you, you have several good alternatives. For parties composed of walkers at different levels of strength and desire, low-level routes are possible for each day. Walkers wishing an easier route can follow Days 2 and 3 of Route 9 Rondane Circle, and Day 4 of Route 7 Rondane Traverse. It is possible to follow the low route on one or all of the 3 days, arriving at the same huts each night as the walkers who choose the high route.

Rondvassbu is a splendid base for the scrambler, and one can ascend Rondslottet (2178m), Vinjeronden (2044m), Veslesmeden (2015m) and Storronden (2138m) from this centre. Storronden is a relatively easy 5-hour round-trip climb, and one of the area's most popular. It makes a fine climb for the beginner, since except for a

Rondvassbu, Rondane

short steep section just below the summit there are no difficult sections to negotiate. Descriptions of the other peak climbs are included in the following route description.

RONDVASSBU (1165m) to BJØRNHOLLIA (914m) via VINJERONDEN (2044m) and RONDSLOTTET (2178m)
8 hours, 18 kilometres

Elevation: Extremely steep, parts moderate
Features: Mountain summit

To start the high route climb the path steeply east up the rocky hill from the hut. After about 10 minutes veer north-west, as the eastern branch takes you to the summit of Storronden. In another ¹/₄ hour you reach a small lake. As you continue eastward toward the low ridge your progress will be slowed by large talus. After reaching the ridge turn north up even steeper slopes. You will reach the summit of Vinjeronden (2044m) approximately 3¹/₂ hours after leaving Rondvassbu. There are fine views toward Rondslottet, Veslesmeden, Storsmeden and the entire Rondane range. Crossing the arête to the summit of Rondslottet looks more difficult than it is, but be sure to follow the trail markers. The Ts mark the eastern side of the ridge since there is a long drop-off to the west. You get a superlative view

94

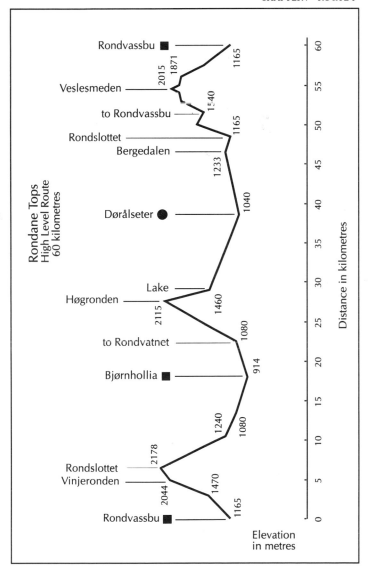

Rondane Tops
High Level Route
60 kilometres

Rondvassbu ■

Veslesmeden

to Rondvassbu

Rondslottet

Bergedalen

Dørålseter ●

Lake

Høgronden

to Rondvatnet

Bjørnhollia ■

Rondslottet

Vinjeronden

Rondvassbu ■

Elevation
in metres

Distance in kilometres

from the top of Rondslottet down into the Storbotn cirque surrounding you, and in fine weather you can see Galdhøpiggen and Glittertind in the Jotunheimen, Norway's two highest peaks.

From the summit follow the cairns across the talus as you descend toward Langglupdalen. Steep at first, the descent levels out as you approach the valley. It will be a bit of a scramble here and there, and may be tiring after your ascent. An hour and a half on the rocks brings you to the turnoff to Dørålseter. Turn south-east at the trail junction towards Bjørnhollia. In about 40 minutes a turnoff to the north veers off to the summit of Høgronden. Another 4 kilometres south and an hour or more walking brings you to the old farm at Bjørnhollia (B/90).

BJØRNHOLLIA (914m) to DØRÅLSETER (1040m) via HØGRONDEN (2115m)
9 hours 15 minutes, 20.5 kilometres

Elevation:	Extremely steep, parts moderate, parts steep
Features:	Mountain summit

Return on yesterday's path up Langglupdalen. After crossing just over 4 kilometres proceed north at the junction toward Høgronden's summit. The western path marks the low-level well marked 7-hour route to Dørålseter (see Route 9 Rondane Circle), and although long, it presents no major obstacles.

Back on the high trail to Høgronden, after taking the north-east alternative at the junction, you will ascend slowly for the next 5 kilometres over talus all the way to the summit. The north-east ridge provides an extremely steep rocky descent for one kilometre, becoming less demanding at about 1700 metres. As you continue to descend you turn west, pass the lake at 1461 metres, and drop below the Midtronden cirque. The moderate trail passes a small lake and crosses the Dørålen about one kilometre before Dørålseter (P/100).

DØRÅLSETER (1040m) to RONDVASSBU (1165m) via VESLESMEDEN (2015m)
7 hours 15 minutes, 21.5 kilometres (High Route)

Rondslottet, 2178 metres, Rondane

Near Breisjøseter, Alvdal Vestfjell
Between Pyttbua and Reindalseter, Tafjord

Terrain:	Almost level, parts steep
Features:	Mountain summit, optional boat service (summer only)

Follow the description above under Route 7 Rondane Traverse from Dørålseter to Rondvatnet. Upon reaching Rondvatnet our high route follows the path south-west up the steep scree slope. At the top of the ridge the trail descends slowly along the top of Rondhalsen. There are fine views to Rondslottet and down to the lake. In an hour you pass the turnoff to the summit of Veslesmeden.

If climbing the peak turn west at the junction and follow the cairns up to the ridge, where after 45 minutes your route flattens out at 1871 metres. Here you walk along a flat area for about one kilometre. In low visibility this may be mistaken for the summit. The trail to the summit ascends steeply from here, and the cairns and trail markers fade a bit, making them difficult to find in fog. Be aware of the dangerous drop-off. From the summit in good weather you can look down into four cirques. Descend the same way you came, and upon reaching the trail junction turn south and continue along the path for 45 minutes, still high above Rondvatnet, to your night's stop at Rondvassbu (B/128).

Route 9: RONDANE CIRCLE
RONDVASSBU to RONDVASSBU
(Low Route)

Distance:	43 kilometres
Time:	3 days
Rating:	Easy
Maps:	Rondane 1718 I, Atnsjøen 1818 IV Rondane 1:100 000
Start Altitude:	Rondvassbu, 1165 metres
Highest Point:	High point below Høgronden, 1418 metres
Base:	Otta
Major Access:	Oslo/Trondheim

RONDVASSBU (1165m) to BJØRNHOLLIA (914m) via ILLMANNDALEN (1280m)
4 hours, 13 kilometres

This low-level route is described under Route 7 Rondane Traverse. A high-level strenuous option is detailed under Route 8 Rondane Tops.

BJØRNHOLLIA (914m) to DØRÅLSETER (1040m)
6 hours 30 minutes, 20 kilometres

Elevation: Parts moderate, parts almost level

Although long, this low route between Bjørnhollia and Dørålseter presents no particular difficulties. To follow the low option from Bjørnhollia head north-west toward Høgronden. The trail affords a slow ascent around the slopes of Veslsvulten, and in 4 kilometres you'll reach the turnoff to the summit of Høgronden. Take a west turn and continue on a more gradual ascent up the Langglupdalen to the day's high point at 1418 metres. Fine views of both Rondslottet to the south, as well as Høgronden and Midtronden to the north, await you. Next, you begin a slow descent to Bergedalen. Before reaching Bergedalen there is a secondary trail that branches north above the river. A short cut to Dørålseter, it is not hard to follow as you remain above the river until it joins the Dørålen turning east. Cross the river about one kilometre before the hut and walk uphill to the two huts (P/100).

DØRÅLSETER (1040m) to RONDVASSBU (1165m) via RONDVATNET (1165m) (by boat)
3 hours, 10 kilometres

This low-level route is described under Route 7 Rondane Traverse, and includes a boat ride across Rondvatnet. Under Route 8 Rondane Tops you'll find a description of a longer moderate route which crosses the northern shore of Rondvatnet, with an optional ascent of Veslesmeden.

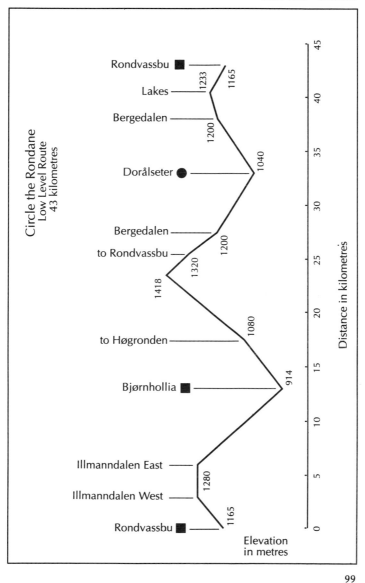

Circle the Rondane
Low Level Route
43 kilometres

Rondvassbu ■
1233
1165
Lakes
Bergedalen
1200
1040
Dorålseter ●
Bergedalen
1200
to Rondvassbu
1320
1418
1080
to Høgronden
914
Bjørnhollia ■
Illmanndalen East
1280
Illmanndalen West
1165
Rondvassbu ■

Distance in kilometres

Elevation
in metres

Route 10: ALVDAL VESTFJELL (Low Route)
Route 11: ALVDAL VESTFJELL (High Route)
FLATSETER TO STRAUMBU

Distance:	24 kilometres (Low Route)
	26 kilometres (High Route)
Time:	2 days
Rating:	Easy (Low Route), Moderate (High Route)
Maps:	Folldal 1519 II, Alvdal 1619 III, Atnsjøen 1818 IV
	Rondane 1:100 000 or Sølnkletten 1:75 000
Start Altitude:	Flatseter, 800 metres
Highest Point:	Gravskardet, 1482 metres (Low Route)
	Sølnkletten, 1827 metres (High Route)
Base:	Alvdal/Røros
Major Access:	Oslo/Trondheim

FLATSETER (800m) to BREISJØSETER (951m) (Low Route)
3 hours, 11 kilometres

Elevation: Almost level

This is a pleasant low-level alternative to the high route described below. From Flatseter head south on the dirt road for 15 minutes, then turn east at the lake at 946 metres. Continue to north of Lake 947 metres. Here take the south branch of the trail between the lakes, both with elevations of 947 metres. The rocky going is compensated by fine views of Sølnkletten. Follow the path south all the way to Breisjøseter (P/48).

FLATSETER (800m) to BREISJØSETER (951m) via SØLNKLETTEN (1827m) (High Route)
4 hours 55 minutes, 13 kilometres

Elevation: Almost level, parts steep
Features: Mountain summit

Under Sølnkletten, Alvdal Vestfjell

Follow the low route directions from Flatseter to the lake at 947 metres. Pass between Veslestertjørna and søre Klettsjøen. Take an unmaintained trail which heads east, although it may be hard to locate. If you have trouble just walk east gradually uphill. In $^1/_2$ kilometre you'll cross a marked trail, the low route from Follandsvangen. Keep walking east and in 5 minutes you come to the high route to Follandsvangen. Turn south and begin an ascent up the north side of Sølnkletten. The trail goes steeply up to the first top at 1690 metres, rewarding you with better and better views of the mountains. You drop down to 1579 metres, and then climb again to the main peak at 1827 metres. Expansive views of the Rondane peaks await you from the top. You descend slowly across talus from the peak's south side. An hour's walk brings you to the farm at Breisjøseter (P/48).

BREISJØSETER (951m) to STRAUMBU (740m) via GRAVSKARDET (1482m)
5 hours, 13 kilometres

Elevation: Moderate, parts steep
Features: Bus (limited service)

101

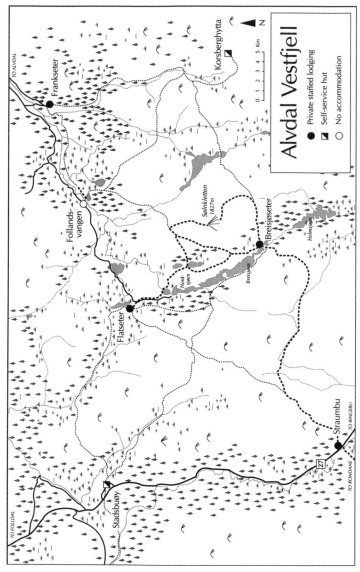

Alvdal Vestfjell

Private staffed lodging ●
Self-service hut ◪
No accommodation ○

0 1 2 3 4 5 Km

N

Korsberghytta

Frankseter

TO ALVDAL

Follands-vangen

Salnkletten
1827m

Breisjøseter

Holmsjøen

Flatseter

Nordsjøen

Breisjøen

Straumbu

TO RINGEBU

TO RONDANE

27

Stadsbuøy

TO FOLLDAL

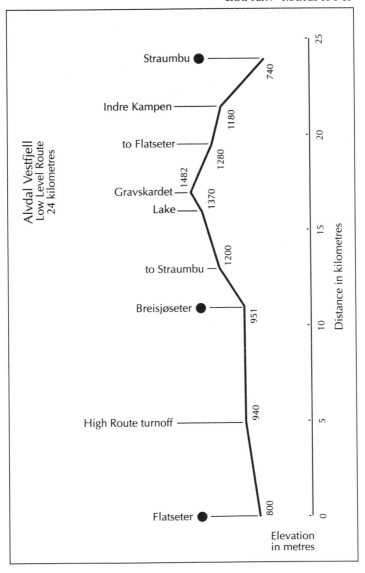

Alvdal Vestfjell
Low Level Route
24 kilometres

Straumbu ●
740

Indre Kampen
1180

to Flatseter
1280

Gravskardet
1482
1370

Lake
1200

to Straumbu

Breisjøseter ●
951

High Route turnoff
940

Flatseter ●
800

Distance in kilometres

Elevation
in metres

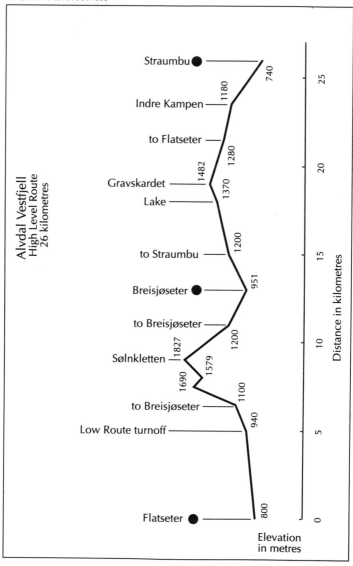

Alvdal Vestfjell
High Level Route
26 kilometres

Straumbu ● — 740

Indre Kampen — 1180

to Flatseter — 1280

Gravskardet — 1482 / 1370

Lake

to Straumbu — 1200

Breisjøseter ● — 951

to Breisjøseter — 1200

Sølnkletten — 1827 / 1579

1690

to Breisjøseter — 1100

Low Route turnoff — 940

Flatseter ● — 800

Elevation in metres

Distance in kilometres

0   5   10   15   20   25

From Breisjøseter take the vehicle road south-west and cross the bridge over the Lona. After 2 kilometres you leave the road at a trail junction where you see our familiar red Ts, turning west on the moderately steep track. Continue moderately uphill to rocky Gravskardet, the obvious gap and high point to the west, which may have snow late into summer. Emerging from the gap, you have fantastic views of the Rondane mountains. As you slowly descend to a rocky plain, you cross a few small streams and in 15 minutes reach the turnoff to Flatseter. Continue west towards Straumbu. From here the descent is gradual, then the trail begins to wind and steepens, and in $1^{1}/2$ hours you meet the trees above Straumbu (P/ 30). To continue to the three Rondane routes, cross the road and bridge for the 2 hour walk to the DNT hut at Bjørnhollia. This will connect with Routes 7, 8, and 9.

STRAUMBU (740m) To BJØRNHOLLIA
2 hours, 6 kilometres

Elevation:	Moderate, parts almost level
Features:	Bus (Straumbu)

From below the hut cross the road and bridge, at first walking westward on flat ground through trees. After 20 minutes the trail goes steeply uphill for 150 metres and then flattens out. Between the pine trees outstanding views of Rondslottet and Høgronden emerge. The track continues southward gradually uphill below Musvolkampen, from where you get your first views of Bjørnhollia and into the gorge below. The track drops steeply down from here and in 10 minutes you meet the old cart track which takes you to Bjørnhollia (B/90).

CHAPTER 8

Western Fjord Ranges

Route 12: TAFJORD
Route 13: DOVRE MOUNTAINS

Wealth I ask not, hope nor love,
Nor a friend to know me;
All I ask, the heaven above
And the road below me.

Robert Louis Stevenson

For organizational purposes here I am presenting the mountain areas of the Dovre and Tafjord together. Both are splendid destinations for the visiting walker, though less well known than the neighbouring Rondane or Jotunheimen. For walkers who prefer self-service huts, less crowded trails and rugged scenery, they are an attractive alternative to the better known touring areas.

Tafjord, along with the Sunnmøre, forms Norway's finest fjord landscape. You'll find this area south-east of the Romsdalen, south of the Trollheimen and west of the Dovre mountains. It is a touring area with much variety, and some consider it Norway's best-kept secret. Deep fjords, mountain valleys, jagged peaks and green-sloped mountainsides highlight the area. One of my favourite trips in Norway combines a walking tour in the Tafjord with a visit to the rock walls of the Romsdal (see Appendix F).

Since 1889 the Sunnmøre Touring Association (ÅST) has maintained a well defined cairned system of paths and routes in the Tafjord. During July and August the ÅST manages two full-service huts, Reindalseter and Kaldhusseter, as well as other self-service and unstaffed cabins.

TRANSPORT
From Oslo or Trondheim take the Dovre railway to Dombås. Change trains for the Romsdal Line to Åndalsnes, getting off at Bjorli. You may wish to call ahead for a taxi to take you on the 30-

Leaving Pyttbua, Tafjord

minute ride from Bjorli to Tunga. A highly recommended detour is to go to Åndalsnes to view the Romsdal and backtrack via train or bus to Bjorli.

You can enter the Tafjord from the west by taking the bus from Åndalsnes to Valldal connecting to Tafjord. This route takes you along the famous Troll's road, Trollstigen. You can then walk this route from east to west, but call ahead for a taxi to pick you up at Tunga.

Route 12: TAFJORD

Distance:	31.5 kilometres
Time:	3 days
Rating:	Moderate
Maps:	Tafjordfjella Turkart 1: 50 000
Start Altitude:	Tunga, 800 metres
Highest Point:	Pass above Lake 1170, 1544 metres
Base:	Åndalsnes/Dombås
Major Access:	Oslo/Trondheim

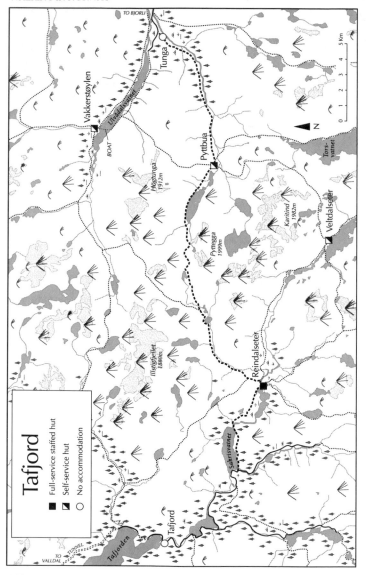

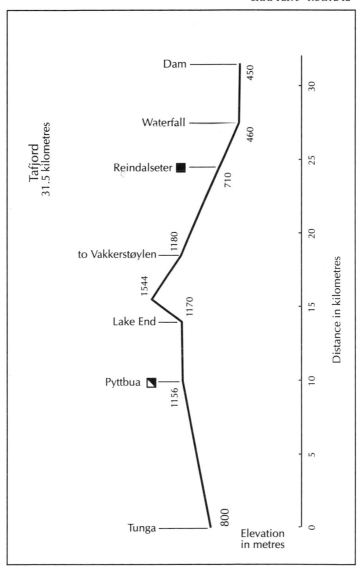

Tafjord
31.5 kilometres

Dam — 450

Waterfall — 460

Reindalseter ■ — 710

to Vakkerstøylen — 1180

1544

Lake End — 1170

Pyttbua ◤ — 1156

Tunga — 800

Elevation
in metres

Distance in kilometres

TUNGA (800m) to PYTTBUA (1156m)
3 hours, 10 kilometres

Elevation:	Gradual
Features:	Taxi (Tunga)

From the parking area at Tunga cross the bridge and proceed west up the narrow dirt road past several summer cabins. After 15 minutes the turnoff to Vakkerstølen continues north. Veer west at the turnoff and walk up the valley, at first in trees, but soon rewarded by fine views of the river below. After 2 hours you gradually leave the trees. You then pass closer to the river, where torrents of water fall into white swollen waves through weathered rocks. Ahead of you the valley is ringed by the high-pointed snowy peaks of Karitind (1982m), Høgstolen (1760m) and Pyttegga (1999m). Three hours from the start you reach the self-service hut Pyttbua (SS/55).

PYTTBUA (1156m) to REINDALSETER (710m) via
HIGH POINT (1544m)
6 hours, 14.5 kilometres

Elevation:	Parts extremely steep, parts gradual, parts moderate
Features:	Mountain pass, mountain views

From Pyttbua walk west up the valley around the north shore of Lake 1170. You will enjoy fine views of high Pyttegga all day. From the lake's western edge follow the Ts up the steep snow slope to the low point in the ridge at 1544 metres. This climb may be snow-covered most of the year; a rope to help you with the climb lies along the slope's south side. From the top you get expansive views of the entire western Sunnmøre peaks. There follows a steep and rocky descent to two lakes below, and after you reach the basin you cross between them. After a 50-metre ascent, you begin a steady descent into the valley. You get stunning views of the high peaks all around. After one hour you bridge the river, and immediately encounter another trail joining from the north and Vakkerstølen.

You remain in the valley for the rest of the day. The green hillsides replace the rocky snow-covered terrain, and contrast beautifully with the pointed peaks that circle your route. You pass north of Lake 1141 through the green Reindalen. You will get good views of Reindalseter (B/93) as you approach the hut from higher up. Just before reaching the hut you'll see the turnoff to Veltdalshytta joining from the east. If you wish to prolong your time in the mountains, head this way tomorrow.

REINDALSETER (710m) to PARKING AREA (450m)
2 hours, 7 kilometres

Elevation:	Parts extremely steep, parts gradual
Features:	Waterfall, bus (at dam)

From the hut head west, around the north shore of Langvatnet. After one hour you begin a very steep descent on a rocky staircase. Below flows a powerful waterfall. Five minutes before you reach the waterfall you cross the river on a bridge. Your last hour follows the north shore of a lake used for hydroelectric power; you'll see the dam at the western end. There is a private summer bus service to/ from Tafjord to the car park. You should ask at Reindalseter for information and call ahead for a reservation.

ALTERNATIVE ROUTES
I have described a route which allows you to enter at one point, Tunga, and exit at the dam above Tafjord and Valldal. If, however, you wish to spend more time in the mountains, a popular route continues east from Reindalseter to Veltdalshytta and then back to Pyttbua. There are cairned routes and huts to the south, however these mountains are not as high or rugged as in the area described, and their landscape has been marred by hydroelectric development.

Route 13: DOVRE MOUNTAINS

Due to roads, the railway, and tourist huts the Dovrefjell National Park is one of the most accessible of all Norwegian national parks. It has long been considered the heart of Norway. In early times Norway "north of the mountains" and "south of the mountains" meant north and south of the Dovre. Some of Norway's oldest travel routes crossed the Dovre. The main road and railway to Trondheim

Unstaffed hut Loennechenbua, Dovre Mountains

go northward through the middle of the park, effectively dividing it into eastern and western sections.

You'll find the Dovre mountain range bordered by the Rondane to the east and Trollheimen to the north. To the far west lie the wild jagged spires of the Romsdal. In the eastern Dovre the undulating Norwegian mountains predominate, but as one walks west the steep and serrated alpine peaks of the Romsdal come into view. In the eastern Dovrefjell one can find marshes and open moors with rounded ridges. West of the railway, and in the area described here, one finds the greatest concentration of high peaks outside the Jotunheimen. Most of the park is above timberline and heights reach to the top of Snøhetta at 2286 metres.

Archaeological findings show us that musk oxen lived in the Dovre mountains during the Ice Ages. Musk oxen from eastern Greenland were released in the Dovre in the 1930s, but killed off during the war. In the late 1940s several were released again, and a healthy herd appears to be thriving. With their thick fur, they are comfortable in winter but dislike warm temperatures. Walkers often encounter musk oxen between Kongsvoll and Reinheim. They are peaceful, but should not be provoked. Since they can weigh up to 400 kilograms their attack can be dangerous, and photographers should never go nearer than 150 metres.

Snøhetta, the main mountain top in the Dovre range, with its beautiful snow-capped mountain ridge and its glacier-filled cirque, is famous throughout Norway's history. As the peak rises up from the Dovre mountain plateau, its isolated and dominant location and its majestic form have brought it notoriety.

TRANSPORT
The Oslo-Trondheim train (Dovre Line) stops at Kongsvoll. At the far end there is a twice-daily bus service from Gjøra and Fale east to Oppdal and west to Sunndalsøra.

Route 13: DOVRE MOUNTAINS

Distance:	60 kilometres
Time:	4 days
Rating:	Moderate
Maps:	Storskrymten 1419 I, Romfo 1420 III, Snøhetta 1519 IV Snøhetta 1:100 000
Start Altitude:	Kongsvoll, 890 metres
Highest Point:	Snøhetta, 2286 metres
Base:	Oppdal
Major Access:	Oslo/Trondheim

KONGSVOLL (890m) to REINHEIM (1340m)
4 hours 15 minutes, 16 kilometres

Elevation:	Gradual, parts moderate
Features:	Train station (Kongsvoll), musk oxen

From the train depot at Kongsvoll (P/50) head directly west through trees and bushes up a steep rocky hill. Gradually as you leave the trees, you will be able to see back to the buildings at Kongsvoll. After 40 minutes a sign marks your entrance to Dovre National Park. The first peak you see is the rounded Kolla, but the impressive three-pointed Snøhetta, which will dominate your views for the next 2 days, soon appears. You head north above the wide river basin, and

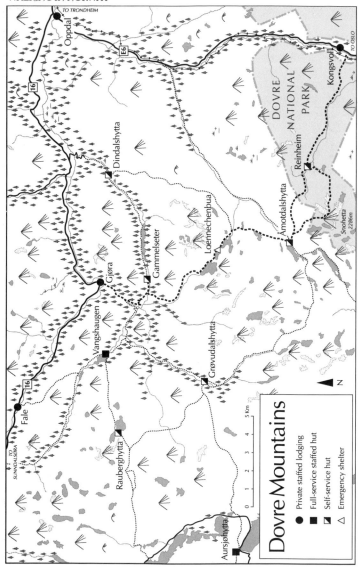

Dovre Mountains

- ● Private staffed lodging
- ■ Full-service staffed hut
- ◩ Self-service hut
- △ Emergency shelter

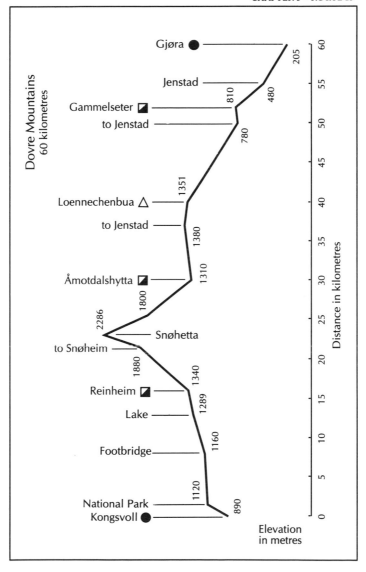

Dovre Mountains
60 kilometres

Distance in kilometres

Gjøra ●
205

Jenstad
810
480

Gammelseter ◨
to Jenstad
780

1351

Loennechenbua △
to Jenstad
1380

Åmotdalshytta ◨
1310
1800

2286

Snøhetta
to Snøheim
1880
1340

Reinheim ◨
1289

Lake
1160

Footbridge

1120

National Park
Kongsvoll ●
890

Elevation
in metres

about 2 hours after your start you cross a creek on a small footbridge. Continue up the Stroplsjødalen and in one hour reach Lake 1289, dotted with summer homes on its western shore. About 60 musk oxen still roam this valley. To the north is a chain of rounded peaks with steep drop-offs into the valley. Continue up the valley to the self-service hut Reinheim (SS/38).

REINHEIM (1340m) to ÅMOTDALSHYTTA (1310m) via SNØHETTA (2286m) (High Route)
6 hours 15 minutes, 14 kilometres

Elevation:	Moderate, parts extremely steep
Features:	Mountain summit, snow crossing

From the hut head south across the creek and start your ascent of Snøhetta. In 40 minutes you'll reach a high flat plateau and pass the first turnoff to Snøheim, an old DNT hut replaced by Reinheim in 1951. Many signposts to it still survive. Looking back, you can see the steep rounded peaks lining the valley you passed through yesterday. To the west the peaks of the Rondane come into view. You now head steadily uphill, more and more on rocks. After about 2 hours you reach another sign and a second turnoff east to Snøheim. You'll then cross snow, reaching the highest summit of Snøhetta in another hour.

Snøhetta is not a true peak, but a long ridge with four peaks in a half circle. The first two peaks, Stortoppen (2286m) and Midttoppen (2278m), are rounded, and the other two, Hettpiggen (2255m) and Vesttoppen (2249m), are sharp. The ridge of this grand peak was once thought to be Norway's highest. Vertical walls from the summit ridge drop down into the Lasbotn cirque. On a clear day the high peaks of the Rondane, Jotunheimen's Galdhøpiggen and Glittertind, Snota in the Trollheimen and the Romsdalhorn are all visible.

To descend follow the red dots and cross in front of the unmanned locked building on the summit. After 30 minutes a short but steep section of snow brings you back to the rocks. Pick your way down over the rocks, and at about 1800 metres your descent becomes more gradual. In the far distance you can make out Åmotdalshytta, your destination for the night. Proceeding down, you again pass the posted route which connects Snøheim with Åmotdalshytta. Finally you meet up with the low route from Reinheim. Turn west and you have one kilometre more to Åmotdalshytta (SS/30).

A 3-hour, 10-kilometre low route connects Reinheim to Åmotdalshytta. From Reinheim the route passes gradually west up the valley, crossing through a low ridge at 1550 metres, and then gradually descending to Åmotdalshytta.

ÅMOTDALSHYTTA (1310m) to GAMMELSETER (810m) via LOENNECHENBUA (1351m)
7 hours 20 minutes, 22 kilometres

Elevation:	Gradual
Features:	Emergency shelter

From Åmotdalshytta follow the Ts along the north-east side of the lake over rocky open areas. As your path continues across expansive rugged country there are good views back to the hut and of yesterday's route to Snøhetta. Next you ascend up a small rise to the east end of Langvatnet and then drop slowly to a river crossing. Here the Ts lead you across a rock bridge to a signpost. Turn east if you are going to Dindalshytta. Our route turns north-west and follows the north shore of the lovely Urdvatnet, where the scenery becomes more alpine. Climb through a rocky notch 100 metres above the lake, and in 10 minutes reach Loennechenbua (U/2), a tiny shelter on the shore of another splendid mountain lake. From here your progress slows as you pick your way along the lake's northern shore around and between large boulders. Now wild rounded peaks are evident to the south-west, and Flaskirådalen opens up to the north. For the next 2 hours you slowly descend into the valley and gradually enter the trees. At about 800 metres you meet a dirt road. Walk along here for about 45 minutes. When you reach the main road a turn west heads you towards Jenstad and tomorrow's route, and a turn east brings you to Gammelseter (SS/22) in 1¹/₂ kilometres. This is an old farm converted to a self-service hut with a fenced-in area to keep the sheep out. A new extension in old Norwegian style has been built to accommodate additional walkers, along with a smaller hut for dogs.

GAMMELSETER (810m) to GJØRA (205m)
2 hours, 8 kilometres

Elevation:	Gradual
Features:	Bus (Gjøra)

From the hut retrace your steps for 20 minutes until you reach the path from Loennechenbua. Turn north and follow the service road down the hill one hour to Jenstad (no service) and past summer homes. Continue now on the paved road one hour into Gjøra, where there is some overnight accommodation, and twice-daily bus service east to Oppdal and west to Sunndalsøra.

ALTERNATIVE ROUTES

As a splendid variation on the above route, head west and north from Åmotdalshytta to the self-service hut Grøvudalshytta. From here continue north to Vangshaugen and Fale. This can be used as an entry/exit point into the Trollheimen. From Gammelseter you can extend your tour for 2 days by continuing directly east to Vangshaugen.

CHAPTER 9

Central Fjord Ranges

Route 14: TROLLHEIMEN TRAVERSE
Route 15: TROLLHEIMEN CIRCLE

The swiftest traveller is he that goes afoot.

Thoreau

Trollheimen, the Home of the Trolls, an area of unsurpassed beauty, boasts of excellent walking within a good framework of huts. The area, less busy than the nearby Rondane or Jotunheimen, is bounded in the south by the Dovre mountains, in the west by the fjords, and in the east by the Rondane. There are several wonderful peaks for walkers including Trollhetta (1616m) and the easier Geithetta (1316m), both directly on the routes described here. Snota (1668m), an arduous but worthwhile climb, considered by some to be the most beautiful in the area, requires an extra day from Trollheimshytta.

In 1890 Trondhjems Tourist Association built its first hut in the Trollheimen, Trollheimshytta. It was many years before hikers recognized the Trollheimen and in 1900 only 21 hikers visited Trollheimshytta. In 1917 the Trondheim Tourist Association built its cabin at Jødalshytta. In 1921 arrangements were made which later led to the hut at Gjevilvasshytta. Trollheimshytta was expanded in 1993.

Innerdalen, one of the most beautiful valleys in Norway, marks a wonderful finale for your visit to the Trollheimen. Innerdalen is a lush stretch of valleys with rivers and lakes encircled by high mountain peaks. In 1973 Innerdalen became a protected area, and the valley's only permanent residents are the family Innerdalen. This is a busy summer rock-climbing centre, with regular DNT courses in progress throughout the season. The scenery here is splendid, although it lacks the isolation of other parts of the Trollheimen. The walks from Kårvatn via Bjøråskardet to Innerdalen and from Innerdalen through Giklingdalen to Fale are some of the most splendid in the country.

119

The first Trollheimen Tour described below, Route 14 Trollheimen Traverse, takes 6 days and crosses west to Innerdalen, the recommended direction for your tour. If you have less time available Route 15 Trollheimen Circle is an excellent choice. This classic though strenuous 3 day tour links Gjevilvasshytta with Jødalshytta, then climbs Trohetta to reach Trollheimshytta and returns to Gjevilvasshytta. An additional advantage is that it uses only huts managed by Trondhjems Turistforening, which like the DNT huts to the south are known for their friendliness, hospitality and true old Norwegian atmosphere.

TRANSPORT

The main base, Oppdal, is easily reached by train on the Oslo-Trondheim (Dovre) Line. Oppdal has hotels, a hostel and limited services. A taxi, available just across the street from the train station, will take you all the way to Gjevilvasshytta, the recommended entrance point. Bus services run to the Festa Bridge (*bru*), but it's still an 11 kilometre walk on the road along the north shore of Gjevilvatnet to the hut. You can also reach Innerdalen from the west from the small town of Ålvundeid, which is served by bus. You must call a taxi to take you from the bus stop to the parking area 4 kilometres from Innerdalen. From Fale at the end of your tour you can continue walking south into the Dovre mountains or catch a bus west to Oppdal or east to Sunndalsøra.

Route 14: TROLLHEIMEN TRAVERSE

Distance:	90 kilometres
Time:	5-6 days
Rating:	Strenuous
Maps:	Snota 1420 I, Romfo 1420 II, Oppdal 1520 III, Trollhetta 1520 IV
	Turkart 1:100 000 Trollheimen
Start Altitude:	Gjevilvasshytta, 700 metres
Highest Point:	Trollhetta, 1616 metres or below Geithetta, 1250 metres
Base:	Oppdal
Major Access:	Oslo/Trondheim

GJEVILVASSHYTTA (700m) to JØLDALSHYTTA (720m) via RIVER MINILLA (900m) and HIGH POINT (1060m)
6 hours, 19 kilometres

Elevation:	Gradual, parts moderate
Features:	River crossing

Gradual ups and downs, splendid scenery and a preview of the Trollhetta and Geithetta peaks mark your relatively easy and straightforward first day. From the hut Gjevilvasshytta (B/54) take the service road north-west one kilometre through the forest, turning right at the junction heading north and uphill. You slowly gain elevation for 1¹/₂ hours, until you break through the forest onto the mountain plateau below Høghøa. As you cross the plateau you pass close to a tarn after 30 minutes (1000m). An additional one hour descent will bring you to the wide shallow River Minilla (900m), which can be forded at the rope. If you want to keep your feet dry you may be able to negotiate the planks on the old bridge 150 metres upstream. After crossing begin the slow gradual ascent to the day's high point at Skrikhøa (1060m) near the reindeer pens. You'll then pass for one hour along the slopes of Gråfjellet, where you can see reindeer. You can see down the valley to Jøldalshytta (B/48), your home for the night. The splendid Trollhetta peaks mark the skyline to the west.

JØLDALSHYTTA (720m) to TROLLHEIMSHYTTA (540m) via TROLLHETTA (1616m) (High Route)
9 hours, 22 kilometres

Elevation:	Extremely steep, parts steep, moderate and almost level
Features:	Mountain peak

Although you have three options for reaching Trollheimshytta, only two are described here. The high route is the most strenuous; it crosses from Jøldalshytta to Trollheimshytta via the Trollhetta summits. The second route, still splendid though less difficult, is described as the second day under Route 15 Trollheimen Circle. It crosses again from Jøldalshytta to Trollheimshytta via Geithetta. The shortest option, not recommended, follows the River Svartådal

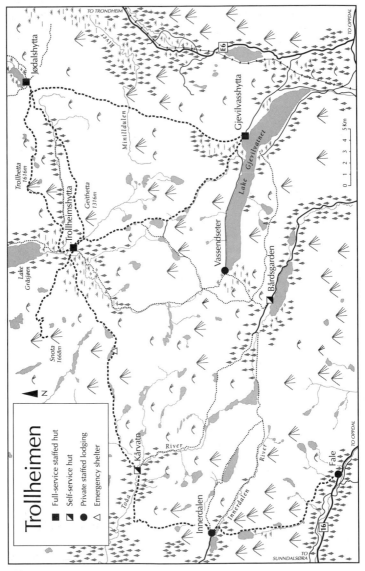

Trollheimen

Full-service staffed hut
Self-service hut
Private staffed lodging
Emergency shelter

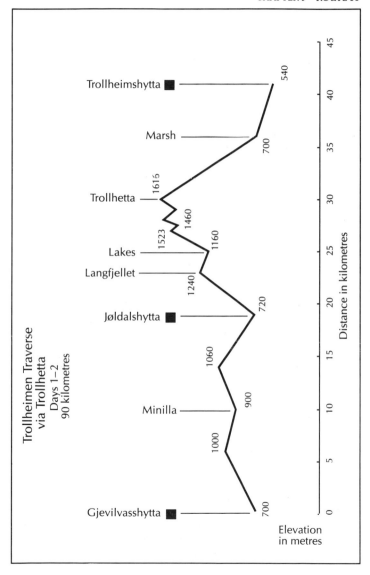

Trollheimen Traverse
via Trollhetta
Days 1–2
90 kilometres

Trollheimshytta

Marsh

Trollhetta — 1615

1460

1523

Lakes — 1160

Langfjellet

1240

Jøldalshytta 720

1060

900

Minilla

1000

Gjevilvasshytta 700

540

700

Distance in kilometres

0 5 10 15 20 25 30 35 40 45

Elevation
in metres

123

for 5 hours. During excessively wet periods or early in the season this route can be very boggy, and since it passes under the high peaks views are limited.

A long but rewarding 8-9 hour route, the first alternative via Trollhetta, is ahead of you. If you are feeling strong and fit follow the River Svartådal on the vehicle road one kilometre west from Jøldalshytta. At the junction turn north-west toward Langfjellet (1240m), ascending 500 metres. Continue west, rising gradually along the ridge to the circle of lakes below the summit of Trollhetta. Follow the loose scree along the edge of the cirque to the first and east summit (1523m). Now negotiate a 30-metre wide ridge followed by another short 60-metre wide ridge as you ascend slowly to the second and north summit (1596m). Now, turning south, you drop about 100 metres and walk 1¹/₂ kilometres to the south summit (1616m). A large cairn on the flat top marks the spot of the highest of the three summits. Enjoy the fine views to Little Hell Lake 500 metres below.

Now that you have reached the summit, a steep descent awaits you. The trail drops sharply south-west from the summit plateau, easier at first when on rock, but harder when you reach the bushes. Finally, after slipping and sliding, you reach the flat marshes and the worst is behind you. The mosquitoes may be numerous here. Continue west through the forest, cross the bridge and you'll arrive at Trollheimshytta (B/55), a little over 2 hours from the south summit.

TROLLHEIMSHYTTA (540m) to KÅRVATN (210m) via HIGH POINT (973m)
8 hours, 22 kilometres

Elevation:	Gradual, parts extremely steep
Features:	Waterfall, shelter

From the hut your long day begins by following the track west through the marsh and across several footbridges over Folla and past the farm Fuglsøysetra. Gradually, you ascend past several lakes and the turnoff to Todalen. To the north the peaks Salen and icy Salsvatnet have snow well into summer. After 5 hours of this gradual ascent you will reach the divide and the day's high point

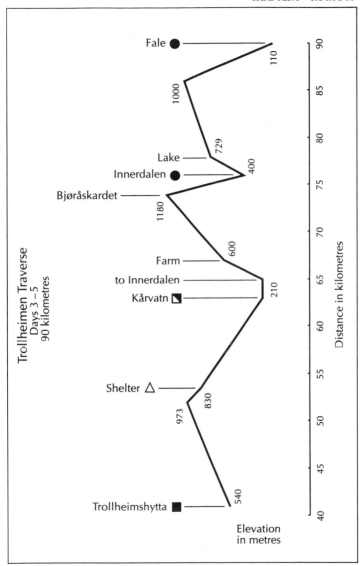

(973m). Twenty minutes later a shelter (830m)(U/2) makes a convenient lunch stop. Just a bit further on fine views of the Todalen mountains await you. Next you begin your 3 hour descent. At first you descend gradually and pass the farm at Naustådalsetra. The descent becomes very steep during the final hour. Take the left fork above Kårvatn and you encounter a lovely two-tiered waterfall. Across the river stands the hut at Kårvatn (SS/19). If the hut is full there may be space at the house next door.

KÅRVATN (210m) to INNERDALEN (400m) via BJØRÅSKARDET (1180m)
5 hours, 13 kilometres

Elevation:	Moderate, extremely steep
Features:	Innerdalen and mountain views

From Kårvatn walk on the surfaced road about 2 kilometres west to the turnoff to Todalen. Turn west uphill at the signpost indicating the path to Innerdalen. The climb is moderate but steady, and in about one hour you will pass an old abandoned farm. Here the trail heads south and continues to climb to a gap between Snøfjellet and Skjerdingfjellet, sometimes over snow. Three and a half hours from Kårvatn you will pass by a large lake to the west, and in another 30 minutes you reach the famous Bruna gap (1180m). The pass blocks the renowned view to the south, so you will not see one of Norway's most spectacular views until you reach the top. From the pass the peaks of Innerdalen are ahead of you: Dalatårnet (the Tower), Skardfjell and Vinnufjell.

Your one hour descent to Innerdalen is rocky and muddy and can be covered with snow. Be careful to look closely for the trail markers, especially in poor visibility. Near the bottom a swimming hole along the river invites you in fair weather. Reindølseter (P/30), a charming old hut with authentic Norwegian atmosphere and excellent food, is located a few minutes north from where the trail meets the road. Turning south at the road you reach Innerdalshytta (P/50) in 10 minutes. This modern hut, built in the late 1980s, and the older building next door make up the centre of the DNT summer rock climbing courses. Both Innerdalshytta and Reindølseter tend to be full during high season, so it is best to call ahead for a

Reindølseter, Innerdalen, Trollheimen

reservation. From Innerdalen it is possible to walk 4 kilometres west down the paved road to the car park, and a taxi, ordered from Innerdalen, can take you to the bus in Ålvundeid.

INNERDALEN (400m) to FALE (110m) via HIGH POINT (1000m) 6 hours, 14 kilometres

Elevation: Moderate, steep
Features: Bus (Fale), entrance to Dovre mountains

After circling the lake south-west of Innerdalshytta you ascend steeply to the west of the waterfall to the west of Storvatn at 700 metres. Huge mountains surround you. The Norsk Alpine Club maintains a hut here for climbers. Continue up the east shore of Storvatn and then west of the smaller Lake Langvatnet. Next you ascend the steep west slope of Såtbakkollen and to the east the views of the peaks continue. After a little over 4 hours you turn east to reach your high point of 1000 metres at the end of the chain of lakes. The steep 2 hour descent into tiny Fale, with bus connections to Sunndalsøra and Oppdal, may at times be tedious. You can continue walking south here to the Dovre mountains and Vangshaugen.

Tour 15: TROLLHEIMEN CIRCLE

Distance:	53 kilometres
Time:	3-4 days
Rating:	Difficult
Maps:	Oppdal 1520 III, Trollhetta 1520 IV
	Turkart 1:100 000 Trollheimen
Start Altitude:	Gjevilvasshytta, 700 metres
Highest Point:	Trollhetta, 1616 metres or Geithetta, 1250 metres
Base:	Oppdal
Major Access:	Oslo/Trondheim

GJEVILVASSHYTTA (700m) to JØLDALSHYTTA (720m) via RIVER MINILLA (900m) and HIGH POINT (1060m)
6 hours, 19 kilometres
This is the first day in Route 14 Trollheimen Traverse and is described above.

JØLDALSHYTTA (720m) to TROLLHEIMSHYTTA (540m) via GEITHETTA (1250m) (Low Route)
6 hours, 18 kilometres

Elevation:	Gradual, parts extremely steep
Features:	Mountain peak

This is a wonderful alternative to the more rigorous route to Trollheimshytta via Trollhetta (see under Route 14 Trollheimen Traverse). Your ascent of Geithetta offers fine views of Trollhetta from across the valley. From Jøldalshytta double back along yesterday's route about one kilometre west down the road past several farms. During the long gradual ascent up the east ridge of Geithetta you get better and better views of the surrounding mountains. For a short period the route flattens out, finally beginning its moderate ascent to the top. The path passes just below the summit of Geithetta at about 1250 metres. A short 15-minute detour south to the obvious summit leads to a good lunch stop. There are fine views to Trollhetta, Snota and Lake Gråsjøen. Now begins the most difficult part of the day as you descend steeply along a rocky

Looking back towards Åmotdalshytta, Dovre Mountains
View from near Gjevilvasshytta, Trollheimen

Gappohytta in the Midnight Sun, Troms Border Trail
Stream crossing along Finnmarksvidda

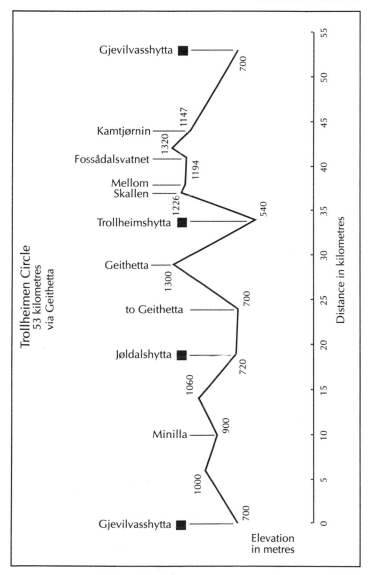

Trollheimen Circle
53 kilometres
via Geithetta

Gjevilvasshytta ■ — 700

Kamtjørnin — 1147
1320
Fossådalsvatnet — 1194
Mellom —
Skallen 1226
Trollheimshytta ■ 540
Geithetta — 1300
700
to Geithetta —
Jøldalshytta ■ 720
1060
900
Minilla — 1000
700
Gjevilvasshytta ■ — 700

Elevation
in metres

Distance in kilometres

0 5 10 15 20 25 30 35 40 45 50 55

View to Snota, Trollheimen

ridge to the valley below. You may have to scramble a bit. Around 2 hours from the summit you come to DNT's isolated Trollheimshytta (B/55).

TROLLHEIMSHYTTA (540m) to GJEVILVASSHYTTA (700m)
8 hours, 19 kilometres

Elevation: Parts steep, parts moderate

This long day rounds out your 3-day tour of the Trollheimen. From Trollheimshytta you make a moderate to steep ascent of the north side of Skallen (1226m). After one hour you break out of the trees and follow the well cairned path as you ascend the ridge with fine views into river valleys on either side. After reaching the first peak your route becomes less steep and the final top is reached at 1320 metres. You then descend slowly to the Mellom lakes, and $1/2$ hour further on is the larger Fossådalsvatnet. After the lake you face a short extremely steep ascent to a pass above the lake's south end. You'll then pass your final two lakes on their eastern shore with steep cliffs on both sides. Then you begin your last slow descent along several river valleys to complete your circuit at Gjevilvasshytta.

CHAPTER 10:
Central Border Mountains

Route 16: SYLENE
Route 17: FEMUNDSMARKA

Give me these hills and the friends I love;
I ask no other heaven

From O'Rourke's Bench Mt. Tamalpais
Marin County, California, USA

East of Trondheim, the Sylene mountains run along the Norwegian-Swedish border for 800 kilometres. Not until the early twentieth century was it finally decided which country owned which summits. In spite of hydroelectric development this popular summer walking area maintains a feeling of wilderness. With its rolling hills and gentle ascents the Sylene presents a contrast to the wild and steep areas to the south. This is an ideal area for people who enjoy long days with easy walking without a great amount of elevation change. Energetic scramblers will find several peaks to their liking.

Trails lace in and out of Sweden and Norway, and you can stay at mountain huts in both countries. English-speaking visitors are few. The Norwegian huts in the Sylene are maintained through Trondhjems Turistforening in Trondheim, where you can get information, topographical and planning maps, transport information, and a key to the self-service huts. You'll find the office of Trondhjems Turistforening just off the town centre area, next to the waterfront and fish market. Swedish huts are maintained by Svenske Turistföreningen in Stockholm. Be sure to show them your DNT card at check-in since DNT members are given a discount on hut charges. The DNT Oslo office has information on the Sylene as well.

Trondheim, a medium-sized town by world standards, is Norway's third largest city and the seat of one of the country's main universities. The Coastal Express, one boat heading north and one heading south, departs twice daily from Trondheim. The Nidaros

Cathedral, parts of which date to the twelfth century, is the city's most famous landmark. Being Norway's coronation cathedral, it houses the crown jewels. The pleasant town centre area, easy to explore on foot, offers the usual assortment of banks, a post office, an outdoor fruit market, supermarkets, hotels and a hostel. Many hotels advertise summer walk-in rates. Outdoor shops stock full supplies for the walker, but quality and choice fall short of what you will find in the larger cities of Oslo or Bergen.

TRANSPORT
You can easily reach Trondheim by plane, or it is a day's trip from Oslo by train, Bergen by bus, or via the coast on the famed Coastal Express. Entrance points to the Sylene mountains are numerous and make travel into the area easy from both Norway and Sweden. A bus from Trondheim links you with Stugudal, approximately 140 kilometres south-east of Trondheim along road 705. You'll find this small town a convenient southern starting point for your tour. To enter the area from the north trains running between Stockholm and Trondheim serve the small towns of Meråker, Storlien and Enafors. From here you can connect to the trail on foot or by taxi.

Route 16: SYLENE

Distance:	93 kilometres
Time:	5-6 days
Rating:	Easy
Maps:	1720 I Stugusjø, 1721 I Meråker, 1721 III Essandsjøen Sylan 1:100 000
Start Altitude:	610 metres
Highest Point:	1380 metres
Base:	Trondheim
Major Access:	Trondheim/Stockholm

STUGUDAL (610m) to NEDALSHYTTA (780m) via VEKTARHAUGEN (780m)
5 hours, 18 kilometres

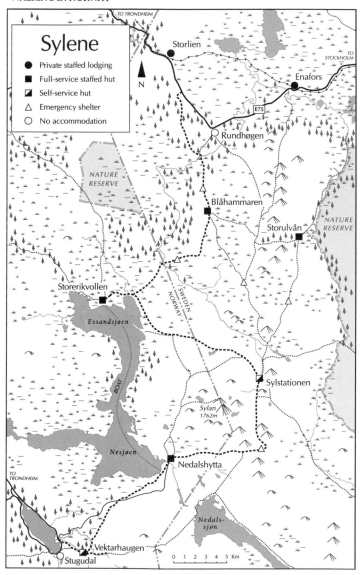

Sylene

- ● Private staffed lodging
- ■ Full-service staffed hut
- ◪ Self-service hut
- △ Emergency shelter
- ○ No accommodation

N

TO TRONDHEIM

Storlien

TO STOCKHOLM

Enafors

E75

Rundhøgen

NATURE RESERVE

Blåhammaren

Storulvån

NATURE RESERVE

SWEDEN
NORWAY

Storerikvollen

Essandsjøen

BOAT

Sylstationen

Sylan
1762m

Nesjøen

Nedalshytta

TO TRONDHEIM

Nedals-
sjøn

Vektarhaugen

0 1 2 3 4 5 Km

Stugudal

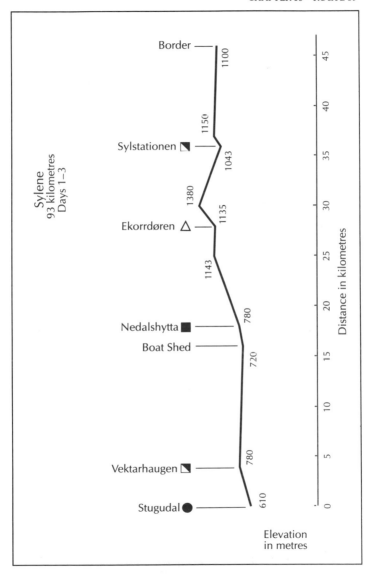

Sylene
93 kilometres
Days 1–3

Border —— 1100

1150

Sylstationen ◪ —— 1043

1380

Ekorrdøren △ —— 1135

1143

Nedalshytta ■ —— 780

Boat Shed —— 720

780

Vektarhaugen ◪ ——

Stugudal ● —— 610

Distance in kilometres

Elevation
in metres

135

| *Elevation:* | Gradual |
| *Features:* | Bus (Stugudal), boat service to Storerikvollen |

From the road between Stugudal and Vektarhaugen, on the eastern end of Stugusjøen, pick up the marked track to Vektarhaugen (SS/7) and walk east for one hour. After the hut follow the track northeast 14 kilometres to Nedalshytta, with fine views to the east to Skarddørsfjella and west to Kjølifjellet. About halfway to the hut the path crosses the road as good vistas out to the lake open up, and you drop gradually to the boat dock. From here walk 2 kilometres on a gradual uphill to Nedalshytta (B/54). If you have a car you can park here. Nedalshytta is a popular starting point for a 3-day circular tour which links up with Sylstationen and Storerikvollen.

NEDALSHYTTA (780m) to SYLSTATIONEN (1043m) via HIGH POINT (1380m)
6 hours 45 minutes, 18 kilometres

| *Elevation:* | Moderate, gradual |
| *Features:* | Shelter/telephone, border crossing into Sweden |

From the hut, take the main path east passing gradually uphill through the trees. On your right to the south, the tall stakes indicate you are paralleling the winter route. After 5 kilometres the path crosses into Sweden, and you can enjoy views back to Lake Nesjøen. Your route continues to rise gradually, until after 3 more kilometres a track veers off south to Nedalssjön. The trail continues to ascend moderately to a winter shelter with a telephone (1135m). Just after the shelter you head north 2 kilometres over a steep rise to the day's high point at 1380 metres. The impressive Sylene peaks to the west distract you as you descend the rocky trail over the next 6 kilometres to the hut. The modern Sylstationen (SNT/90/store/sauna), with several wings and a central self-service kitchen, replaced a previous hut that burnt down a few years ago. You can use your Norwegian money, though at a rate advantageous for the Swedes. During the high summer season scrambling tours of the Sylene peaks are offered from the hut.

You will notice that trail markers differ between the two countries. The Swedish trail markings are not the familiar T markings of

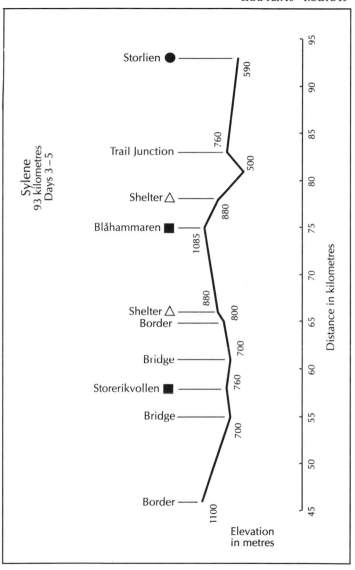

Sylene
93 kilometres
Days 3 – 5

Storlien ● — 590

Trail Junction — 760 500

Shelter △ — 880

Blåhammaren ■ — 1085

Shelter △ — 880

Border — 800

Bridge — 700

Storerikvollen ■ — 760

Bridge — 700

Border — 1100

Distance in kilometres

Elevation
in metres

Norway's DNT. Large red dots up to 30 centimetres wide, in the centre of rocks, mark summer walking routes in Sweden. Stakes for winter routes stand up to about 3 metres with two wooden planks placed at right angles just below the top of the pole.

SYLSTATIONEN (1043m) to STORERIKVOLLEN (760m) via HIGH POINT (1150m)
6 hours, 22 kilometres

Elevation:	Rolling, gradual
Features:	Shelter/telephone, border crossing into Norway, boat service

From the hut cross the bridge to the true left of the river. Continuing west it takes about 20 minutes to climb up a moderate slope to the day's high point at 1150 metres. Then begin a 3-hour rolling traverse of the north slope of Vaktklumpen continuing all the way to the Norwegian border (1100m). Here a fence marks the crossing at the stile, and a small locked building sits about 20 metres after the border.

Descend slowly over the next 12 kilometres, taking care to follow the markers for the summer route, which after 4 kilometres diverges east from the winter route. The trail becomes boggy as you descend lower into the marsh. Early in the season wooden planks make the going much easier. The trail wanders around the eastern edge of Essandsjø and crosses a bridge 3 kilometres before the hut. Continue north and then east along the flat marshes to Storerikvollen (B/65), a quaint old hut. Day trips are possible to the top of Remskleppen (928m) and a one kilometre walk takes you to the dock for the summer boat service to Nedalshytta.

STORERIKVOLLEN (760m) to BLÅHAMMAREN(1085m)
5 hours, 17 kilometres

Elevation:	Gradual
Features:	Shelter/telephone, border crossing into Sweden, Sweden's highest mountain hut

From Storerikvollen follow the wooden planks east across the marsh backtracking around 3 kilometres from the previous day's walk. Just beyond the bridge you pass a turnoff south to Nedalshytta, a 7-hour walk in all. To continue north-west on to Blåhammaren, now on the west slopes of Remskleppen (928m), you cross over a rise which affords enjoyable views to the west and pass two small tarns. After 7 kilometres you enter Sweden again and almost immediately cross a bridge. Within 20 minutes and one kilometre you will come to a winter emergency shelter (telephone). The large high outside bell is rung by the wind during a winter storm and guides lost skiers to the shelter. From here a gradual uphill ascent follows all the way to Blåhammaren, today's high point (1085m) (SNT/28/store/limited provisions) and Sweden's highest mountain hut. Both full-service and self-service facilities are available.

BLÅHAMMAREN(1085m) to STORLIEN(590m)
5 hours, 18 kilometres

Elevation:	Moderate
Features:	Shelter/telephone, Sweden's highest mountain hut, bus/train/taxi service (Storlien)

There are several choices today for your exit. This route goes north gradually leaving the mountains and passes a shelter at around kilometre 7. About 4 kilometres past the shelter the trail forks just after a bridge (500m). The east fork takes you to Rundhøgen (610m) where you can arrange for a taxi pick-up by calling ahead from Blåhammaren. The west fork after the bridge takes you through a marshy area, gradually climbs to a rise (760m) and then descends to a small town, Storvallen. To reach Storlien, with excellent bus and train connections to Trondheim and Stockholm, walk west along the road another 4 kilometres.

BOAT SERVICE
In the summer a regular boat service on Lake Essandsjøen links Nedalshytta and Storerikvollen.

ALTERNATIVE ROUTES
From Storerikvollen you can head west to Ramsjøhytta and Schultzhytta. If you explore this western area you will need the key to the self-service huts available from Trondhjems Turistforening.

Route 17: FEMUNDSMARKA

The Femund mountain area, just south of the Sylene, is bounded by the Swedish border in the east and the Østerdal in the west. Femundsmarka, named after Lake Femund, was declared a Norwegian National Park in 1971. This wide-open flat moorland, dotted with lakes and famous for its trout, is broken only by a few bare peaks rising above the mountain plateau. Lake Femund, in the centre of the park, is 59 kilometres long and covers 202 square kilometres. The old steamer *Femund II* traverses the lake in the summertime.

Gutulia National Park, a 19 square kilometre section in the south-east part of Femundsmarka, was established in 1968. Spruce and pine grow in the park, along with 230 kinds of vascular plants. This area is rich in fauna when compared with the rest of Femundsmarka: reindeer, badger, teal and golden eagle can be seen. There are no marked paths or accommodation inside Gutulia.

Visiting Femund, the seventeenth-century copper mining town of Røros on UNESCO's World Heritage list, makes a unique overnight stop prior to reaching the mountains. Much of the old town, with its 250-year-old homes, church and mine, has been preserved. The last mine did not close until 1986.

Due to the their easterly location both Femund and the Sylene generally receive less winter snow than walking areas to the west. As a result they are often open to walkers by the end of June. However, in Femundsmarka mosquitoes can be a nuisance in the early season.

TRANSPORT
To reach Femundsmarka take the bus or train (Oslo-Trondheim: Røros Line) to Røros. Catch the morning bus to Sørvika and the boat to Røoset, where you begin your walk. When finished take the afternoon boat from Elgå to Femundstunet and from here bus service links you to Oslo and Trondheim.

Distance:	28.5 kilometres
Time:	2 days
Rating:	Easy
Maps:	Røa 1719 I, Elgå 1719 II
	Nordre Femund 1:100 000, Søndre Femund 1:100 000
Start Altitude:	Røoset, 660 metres
Highest Point:	Falkfangarhøgda, 960 metres
Base:	Røros
Major Access:	Oslo/Trondheim

RØOSET (660m) to SVUKURISET (819m) via FALKFANGARHØGDA (960m) and RØVOLLEN (709m)
5 hours 45 minutes, 19.5 kilometres

Elevation:	Almost level
Features:	Boat (Røoset)

From the boat dock at Røoset head east remaining north of the River Røa in the pine trees. Cross into the National Park after 20 minutes, and after 40 minutes more you reach the hut Røvollen (SS/21), pleasantly situated about one kilometre west of the main lake. From the hut continue east, past the turnoff which heads east into Sweden, until you reach the lake and cross the river on a bridge veering south-west. Proceed up the small hill east of Svarttjørn, continuing south in the birch trees. Eventually as you gain 50 metres of altitude you emerge from the birch trees onto the flat moors. Four kilometres from the bridge you come to a series of large lakes. This area tends to be marshy and in early season can have a lot of mosquitoes. Continue directly south across this featureless plateau east of Falkfangarhøgda. Svukuriset (B/43) is 5 kilometres further south from your high point at 960 metres.

SVUKURISET (819m) to ELGÅ (662m)
3 hours, 9 kilometres

Elevation:	Gradual, almost level
Features:	Boat service (near Svukuriset and Elgå)

If you wish to pick up the boat, the dock is a one hour walk west

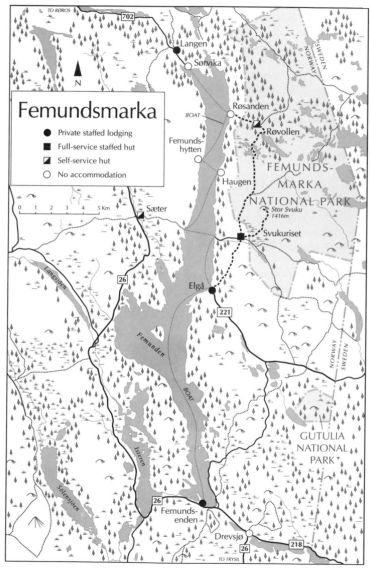

TO RØROS

702

Langen

Sørvika

N

Femundsmarka

● Private staffed lodging

■ Full-service staffed hut

▨ Self-service hut

○ No accommodation

0 1 2 3 4 5 Km

Røsanden

BOAT

Røvollen

Femunds-
hytten

Haugen

FEMUNDS-
MARKA

NATIONAL PARK

Stor Svuku
1416m

Sæter

Svukuriset

SWEDEN

NORWAY

26

Elgå

221

Feemunden

Langsjøen

BOAT

NORWAY

SWEDEN

Isteren

GUTULIA

NATIONAL

PARK

Sølensjøen

26

Femunds-
enden

Drevsjø

26

218

TO TRYSIL

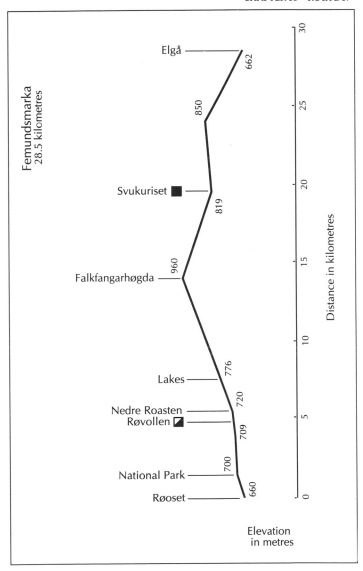

Femundsmarka
28.5 kilometres

Elgå — 662

850

Svukuriset ■ — 819

Falkfangarhøgda — 960

Lakes — 776

Nedre Roasten — 720

Røvollen ◪ — 709

National Park — 700

Røoset — 660

Distance in kilometres

30

25

20

15

10

5

0

Elevation
in metres

down the road from the hut. Our walking route continues south through the pine trees to a lake, and then gradually uphill to a low gap below Gråvola and Sandtjørnvola. You enter the trees again as you walk gradually downhill and proceed through a pine and birch forest all the way to the boat launch. Here you again pick up the *Femund II* heading south to Femundstunet. Buses link up with the boat, providing same-day connections to Oslo and Trondheim.

BOAT SERVICE
There is summer boat service on Lake Femund on the old streamer *Femund II*. It links Sørvika with Røoset, Femundshytta, Haugen, Jonasvollen, the boat dock west of Svukuriset, Elgå and Femundstunet.

ALTERNATIVE ROUTES
It is possible to enter Femundsmarka from the railway station at Tynset, and by walking east, hook up with the self-service huts of Knausen, Raudsjødalen and Ellefsplass. You can cross Femunden at Jonasvollen and reach the described route in the south at Svukuriset. Other trails lead eastward into Sweden.

CHAPTER 11:
Mid-Norway

Route 18: MOUNTAINS OF NARVIK

The journey not the arrival matters.

T.S. Eliot

The Mountains of Narvik, as described here, are bounded on the north by the Swedish railway, in the east and south-west by the Swedish border, and by the fjords to the west of the city. Most visitors are local people. Tourists in the mountains come largely from nearby Finland and Sweden, a few from southern Norway, and a rare visitor from more distant parts of Europe.

Narvik, approximately 300 kilometres north of the Arctic Circle and 1483 kilometres north of Oslo, beautifully situated below the mountains, was established around the turn of the century as an ice-free port for exporting Swedish iron ore. The necessary tangle of railway tracks may to some mar its natural beauty. To help overcome that impression take the cable car up the Fagernestoppen (1270m) and see the Midnight Sun. Narvik is also a winter downhill ski centre. The mountains around Narvik and the Troms Border Trail (Route 19) are popular with cross-country skiers. A bus trip to Narvik from either Tromsø or Bodø or the train from Sweden will help you appreciate the scenery.

On 7 May 1940 Germany invaded Norway through Narvik. The occupying forces stayed for more than 5 years. Narvik, levelled by bombing, has been completely rebuilt. The War Memorial Museum, located in the town centre, uses fascinating pictures and models to chronicle the city during the war.

Narvik Og Omegn Turistforening (NOT) dates from the turn of the century when tourists first came to see the iron mines. The possibilities for mountain walking were soon realized and trails were marked to Fagernestoppen, Totta and Den Sovende Dronning (the Sleeping Queen). NOT is now an organization of mountain walkers. Their first hut, Stordalsstua, was built in 1933. This hut and others were burnt down during the war. For the city of Narvik and for NOT rebuilding marked the postwar years.

Today's huts were built one by one over the succeeding years. Winter storms and flooding have made it necessary to move or rebuild several of them. In the early 1980s the organization began to build a chain of huts with connecting cairned tracks. Narvik Og Omegn Turistforening now manages 17 huts in 9 locations.

The huts along this route are all unstaffed, but are clean and nicely appointed. They are fully equipped with bedding, gas, pots and pans and kitchen utensils. You need only a sheet-sleeping bag. When I visited this area the huts used the standard DNT key. Do not fail to pick up your key at the touring office at the Narvik fire station, just off the main city square. Make sure the standard DNT key still applies.

MAPS
The maps in the M711 series are out of date, and not all the trails are included. The Narvik-Abisko 1:100 000 map is current, but drawn to a larger scale.

TRANSPORT
You may choose among several ways to reach Narvik. The easiest and most efficient way is via daily flights from all major southern Norwegian cities, with connections from Bodø. You can walk into town from the city airport. A less expensive choice is to fly directly to Evenes, about one hour from Narvik, and take the airport bus into town. If you prefer the train take the Norwegian Northern Line from Trondheim to Bodø. Get off at Fauske and catch the bus to Narvik, or take the Swedish train from Stockholm. There are also several buses a day from northern cities such as Tromsø.

Route 18: MOUNTAINS OF NARVIK

Distance:	80 kilometres
Time:	5 days
Rating:	Moderate
Maps:	Bjørnfjell 1431 I, Čunojávri 1431 II, Skjomdalen 1431 III. Narvik 1431 IV

	Narvik - Abisko 1:100 000
Start Altitude:	Katterat, 400 metres
Highest Point:	Rienatvággi, 1116 metres
Base:	Narvik
Major Access:	Tromsø/Trondheim

KATTERAT (400m) to HUNDDALSHYTTA (700m) via LANGRYGGEN (780m)
3 hours 30 minutes, 13 kilometres

Elevation: Moderate, parts extremely steep
Features: Railway station (Katterat)

From Narvik take the Swedish train east, getting off after about 30 minutes at Katterat, just before the border. The high route to Hunddalshytta starts across the tracks from the station where a ladder climbs a steep embankment to the trail. (The low route along the road is described as Day 5.) Go up through the trees and after about one hour break out into the open to the top at Hunddalstoppen (721m). Fifteen minutes further along, you reach the day's high point at Langryggen at 818 metres. Another ¹/₂ hour brings you to a pleasant chain of lakes. Looking back towards your start you see the railway with its many tunnels winding through the mountains. Two waterfalls, known as the Twin Sisters, appear on the rocky ridge to the north of the railway. For one hour you walk along this mountain ridge, twisting up and down near several tarns and then finally dropping down to a gravel road. It is one hour along the road to the two huts at Hunddalshytta (U/14), about 10 minutes past the private hut at the dam (not on the M711 map). These two huts are beautifully situated at the head of two valleys with splendid views of surrounding mountains and glaciers.

HUNDDALSHYTTA (700m) to ČUNOJÁVRI (709m)
6 hours, 18 kilometres

Elevation: Moderate, extremely steep
Features: Shelter, river crossing (optional)

To begin your day it is easiest to backtrack to the private hut and

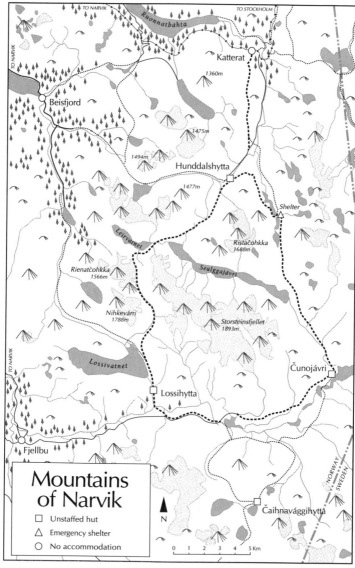

Mountains of Narvik

☐ Unstaffed hut
△ Emergency shelter
○ No accommodation

N

0 1 2 3 4 5 Km

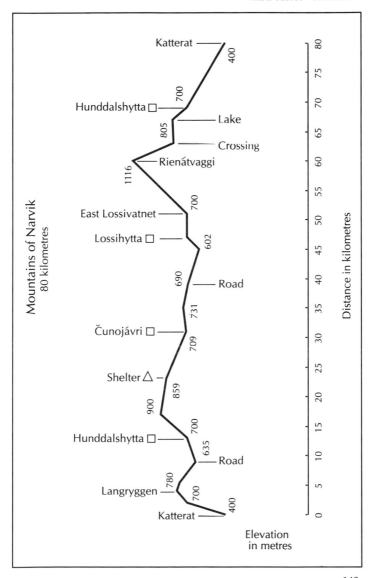

Mountains of Narvik
80 kilometres

Katterat — 400
700
Hunddalshytta □ —
Lake
805
Crossing
1116
Rienátvaggi
700
East Lossivatnet —
Lossihytta □ — 602
690
Road
731
Čunojávri □ — 709
Shelter △ —
859
900
Hunddalshytta □ — 700
635
Road
780
Langryggen —
700
Katterat — 400

Distance in kilometres

Elevation
in metres

149

cross the river at the dam. If you prefer to cross near the hut you will have to ford the river. A cairned route starts on the other side of the dam on the river's true right, circling north-east around the northern slope of Peak 1169. Heading on the rocky track you circle the peak and then head south, high above the river valley, along the snowy lower slopes of Ristacohkka. The day's high point at 900 metres comes after $1^{1/4}$ hours. This route is marked as a secondary trail on the M711 (1431 I Bjørnfjell) map. Next you slowly descend to the river valley, walking on the river's true left, passing over numerous stream outlets until finally you cross the river, south-west of the outlet of Lake 852. Next head north for 15 minutes and then turn south again. Look closely for the shelter, just north of the trail, east of where the secondary trail joins the main trail from the north and north of Lake 852. Now you head south in the Oallavággi valley below steep slopes on both sides of the lake. Your route for the rest of the day is not difficult as you pass along the eastern shores of Lakes 852 and 858. Even steeper slopes mark the western side of your route as you pass below Bálggesvárri. In a little over one hour you break out of the river valley and approach the large Lake Sealggajávri. Continue south on the outlet's true left, following it all the way down the valley. Views of the splendid Storsteinsfjellet beautify your walk along the River Sealggajávri to the huts Čunojávri (U/13).

ČUNOJÁVRI (709m) to LOSSIHYTTA (700m) via HIGH POINT (731m)
5 hours, 16 kilometres

Elevation:	Moderate
Features:	Road

From the huts head west on the track under the shadow of the snowy slopes of Storsteinsfjellet. This is a lovely river valley and you stay on the river's true right for the entire day. After about 4 kilometres you reach the day's high point at 731 metres, and a traverse brings you to a road which mars the splendid alpine scene. It is possible to continue down this road for several more hours to Fjellbu and Bogholmen, where there is a summer bus service into Narvik. Walk west down the road for almost 2 hours to the turnoff to Lossihytta, and turn north. In 45 minutes, after crossing the river on a bridge, you'll reach Lossihytta (U/10).

LOSSIHYTTA (700m) to HUNDDALSHYTTA (700m)
8 hours, 22 kilometres

Elevation:	Moderate, parts steep
Features:	River crossing

This makes for a long and tiring day, but includes superlative mountain scenery. From Lossihytta take the track north along the eastern shore of Lossivatnet. As you reach the lake's north-east end the track splits and your route continues east. This trail is not included on the M711 (1431 III Skjomdalen) map; it appears on the Narvik-Abisko 1:100 000 map. An uncairned route leads west into Beisfjord. Our route goes north between the snowy slopes of Storsteinsfjellet, Nihkevárri and Rienatčohkka. In the distance Leirvatnet finally comes into view, and you descend slowly to the lake's south-eastern shore. At the lake outlet a difficult crossing awaits you. Look carefully for the best place to cross. This may lie to the east of the small lake, 200 metres to the east of the true lake outlet. Now you are well below the fine peaks of Sealggačohkka. Passing down your next river valley, you complete your circle back to Hunddalshytta.

HUNDDALSHYTTA (700m) to KATTERAT (400m)
3 hours, 11 kilometres

Elevation:	Gradual
Features:	Road, railway (Katterat)

If you want the quickest way back to the railway, you can walk on the road. As you leave the high peaks behind, the dirt road gradually descends the valley all the way to the railway station at Katterat. You may wish to delay your return to civilization by retracing your steps on the high route described under Day 1.

ALTERNATIVE ROUTES
From Čunojávri it is possible to head south around the west side of Čaihnavárri to Čaihnavággihyttene. Continue up the western edge of these remote mountain peaks to join the road to Bogholmen and Lossihytta as described above.

CHAPTER 12:
Arctic Norway

Route 19: TROMS BORDER TRAIL

Thou canst not stir a flower
Without troubling of a star.

Francis Thompson

Known as "Norway's Last Wilderness", the Troms Border Trail winds through the valleys of Dividal, Rostadal and Signaldal west of the Finnish and Swedish borders, and through the Øvre Dividal National Park. Though isolated the route described is remarkably well marked and well cared for throughout its length. In summer you can wander about, sleeping in unstaffed huts and have the mountains to yourself.

Tromsø, the most important city north of the Arctic Circle, makes an excellent starting point for your walk. The surrounding mountains reach 1800 metres and the Midnight Sun shines between 21 May and 23 July. Known for its night life, the "Paris of the North" is home to one of Norway's major universities. Attractions include the Arctic Cathedral, the cable-car that whisks you to the top of the mountains outside the city and the Polar and Tromsø museums, which give you an idea of local history and Sami culture.

In summer the weather in northern Norway is often remarkably mild. Although mountain weather can change abruptly, the sun may shine continuously for days on end. Mosquitoes may be your most frequent companions; river crossings are the greatest hazard. A walking stick is recommended for river crossings.

Troms Turlag manages all the huts, and prefers that you deposit the fees for your stay in their post office account. If unable to do that you can leave your money in the hut cash box. You will find keys, issued only to DNT members, at several locations in Tromsø and Sætermoen. This includes some service stations, the local touring offices and tourist offices. Call ahead to Troms Turlag for specific information.

The Nordkalottruta, described in a DNT leaflet, opened in 1991. This 800 kilometre long distance walking path cuts through northern sections of Norway, Sweden and Finland. The "borderless walk" features 40 overnight stays at mountain huts with a reasonable day's walk between stops. On the Troms Border Trail the section between Rostahytta and Innset is part of the Nordkalottruta. From Rostahytta the Nordkalottruta heads east into Finland at Treriksrøysa, the point where Finland, Sweden and Norway intersect. From the western side at Innset the route continues south into Sweden to Lappjordhytta. The DNT issues a brochure on the walk.

MAPS
The 1:100 000 Indre Troms map, updated in 1983, provides topographical detail on Norway, Sweden and Finland. The M711 maps are very old and some trails are omitted. Sweden and Finland are blank on these Norwegian maps.

TRANSPORT
The route, described from east to west, can be walked easily in either direction; transport is good to both ends. Flights go to Tromsø, 240 kilometres north of Narvik, from all major Norwegian cities. Be sure to look for the special SAS summer rates. Round-trip air fares can be less than the train rates. If you prefer the train take the Northern Line north from Trondheim, alight at Fauske and connect with one of the buses along the E6 to Narvik and Tromsø.

From Tromsø a Finnish bus travels along the E8 to the Norwegian-Finnish border for the 2¹/₂ hour ride to just north of Kilpisjärvi. Get off the bus about one kilometre before the Finnish border; you can see the familiar DNT trail markers from the road. Remember, as you study the Finnish timetable, that Finland is 2 hours ahead of Greenwich mean time (GMT) and one hour ahead of Norwegian time. If your bus driver speaks only Finnish you may have to show him on your map where you want to get off.

On the western end your walk ends in Innset, a hamlet with a limited service to Sætermoen. The once-a-week morning bus service takes the summer residents of Innset into town for their shopping. You may prefer to call a taxi for the 30-minute ride into town.

Before Isdalen, Troms Border Trail

Sætermoen, located along the E6 between Tromsø and Narvik, is a small town with a supermarket, bus and taxi service and accommodation. If starting in the west, last minute supplies can be purchased here. Once in Sætermoen buses run several times a day along the E6 south to Narvik and north to Tromsø. The tourist office in Sætermoen can provide you with a bus timetable to and from Innset.

If travelling west to east take the bus north along the E6 north from Narvik or south from Tromsø to Sætermoen. The easiest way to Innset is by taxi. If you are lucky, or if you've planned ahead, you may be able to catch the weekly shopping bus back into Innset in the afternoon.

From the eastern end of the route on the E8, a Finnish bus heads north to Tromsø and south into Finland. Walk north from Gåldahytta as described below to the point where the trail meets the road. You may have to signal the bus to stop for you.

Route 19: TROMS BORDER TRAIL

Distance:	141 kilometres
Time:	8 days
Rating:	Moderate
Maps:	1532 II Altevatn, 1532 III Salvasskardet, 1632 III Julusvarri, 1633 II Helligskogen, 1633 III Signaldalen, 1634 IV Rostadalen 1:100 000 Indre Troms
Start Altitude:	520 metres, Galgujav'ri
Highest Point:	Gap before Rostahytta, 1001 metres
Base:	Tromsø/Narvik/Sætermoen
Major Access:	Tromsø/Narvik

GALGUJAV'RI (520m) to GÅLDAHYTTA (527m) via HIGH POINT (930m)
4 hours, 14 kilometres

Elevation:	Moderate, parts gradual
Features:	Bus (Galgujav'ri), Treriksrøysa (border crossing of Norway, Sweden and Finland)

You should get off the bus about one kilometre north of the Finnish border, where you can see the red DNT trail markers. The M711 map places this stop at $1^{1}/_{2}$ kilometres before the border, but the Indre Troms map shows it to be only $^{1}/_{2}$ kilometre before the border. The large islands to the west in the middle of Lake Galgujav'ri provide a helpful general marker.

The trail proceeds level at first. An hour's walk brings you to the base of your first climb, a short but steep 60-minute pull up towards Goallarras'sa. The route then runs high in a rocky mountain environment with outstanding views back towards the large Finnish lakes. At the crest of the hill you drop about 50 metres and pass between two mountain lakes at 843 and 832 metres. Admire the view across the broad river valley towards the high peaks of Gallagai'bi and Vassdalstind. Next descend from the top to west of

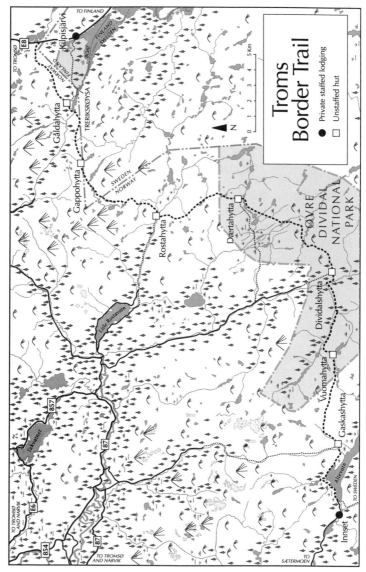

Troms
Border Trail

● Private staffed lodging
□ Unstaffed hut

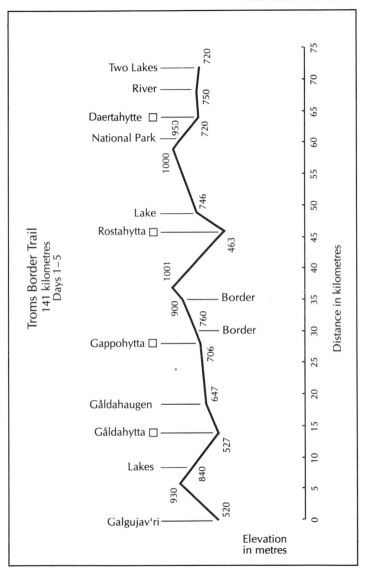

Troms Border Trail
141 kilometres
Days 1–5

Two Lakes — 720
River — 750
Daertahytte ☐ — 720 / 950
National Park — 1000
746
Lake —
Rostahytta ☐ — 463
1001
Border
900 / 760
Border
Gappohytta ☐ — 706
647
Gåldahaugen —
Gåldahytta ☐ — 527
Lakes — 840
930 / 520
Galgujav'ri —

Distance in kilometres

0 5 10 15 20 25 30 35 40 45 50 55 60 65 70 75

Elevation
in metres

Galdabak'ti and on to the two huts at Gåldahytta (U/20).

Most of the overnight stops along the route have two huts, similarly laid out. They lock with a key from Troms Turlag. Characteristically, one hut is old; the other recently built. Equipment includes a stove for heat, a gas stove for cooking, utensils, pots and pans and blankets.

Pictures of the King's visit to the hut during the inauguration of the Nordkalottruta line the walls at Gåldahytta.

It is 3 kilometres from Gåldahytta to the Three Borders (*Treriksrøysa*) where Norway, Sweden and Finland meet. You can walk to the monument the same day you arrive at Gåldahytta and return for the night. When the borders were remeasured a few years ago, the point of true crossing was found to be in the middle of the lake. Walkways are provided out to the ugly yellow floating monument. An older monument located on land is in poor repair.

If walking west to east you can pick up a boat to Kilpisjärvi from Treriksrøysa, and then catch the afternoon bus north to Tromsø. Boats run only in good weather. The walk from the monument to Kilpisjärvi takes 3 hours. There is a Finnish hut at the monument; you must have a full sleeping bag and all your food.

GÅLDAHYTTA (527m) to GAPPOHYTTA (706m) via GÅLDAHAUGEN (647m)
4 hours, 14 kilometres

Elevation: Moderate, parts gradual, parts almost level

This is another short but spectacular day. From Gåldahytta head west to the lake outlet. To the north-west the pyramidal Paras peak looms, and to the north-east you'll see Mar'kus and the chain of high ragged peaks that form the eastern boundary of the Signadalen valley. After crossing the river outlet you climb slightly to just below Gåldahaugen. Now for an hour you move westward along a high mountain ridge past a chain of lakes. After another kilometre you wind through a group of mountain tarns and may see reindeer. The wild peaks to the north-west are closer now, imparting the true sense of the remoteness of these mountain ranges. Crossing up and down several steep river banks, you come to the two huts at Gappohytta (U/20). High peaks surround you in this splendid mountain location.

GAPPOHYTTA (706m) to ROSTAHYTTA (463m) via HIGH POINT (1001m)
6 hours, 18 kilometres

Elevation:	Moderate, parts gradual
Features:	Border crossing into Sweden and back into Norway, river crossings

This is another outstanding day with scenery that matches yesterday's. Leave the hut and head south-west. Don't be confused by the winter trail leading south; a compass reading will be helpful. Head west across the plateau and in 45 minutes cross into Sweden.

Now begins some of the most impressive parts of this entire trail. The views to the west are splendid with high peaks, ragged spires, and icy lakes ahead of you. After one hour and 15 minutes cross back into Norway and enter Isdalen, the Ice Valley. The valley narrows and icy blocks float conspicuously in the lakes. After a total of $2^{1/2}$ hours on the trail you come to a good lunch spot opposite Isdalfjella at the south end of Lake 904.

Continue slowly through the valley to the high point of the entire route at 1001 metres. There are splendid views back into the Ice Valley with fine panoramas of several mountain ranges. A gradual 3 hour descent follows. First you pick your way over rocks, slowly moving from marker to marker. Gradually more and more grass appears underfoot and you leave the winter-like scenes of the Ice Valley far behind you. As you move south high peaks rise to the east. Finally you come to a river valley with Mås'kanvarri towering above you. The two huts at Rostahytta (U/20) are pleasantly located next to the river.

ROSTAHYTTA (463m) to DÆRTAHYTTA (720m) via HIGH POINT (1001m)
5 hours 30 minutes, 18 kilometres

Elevation:	Gradual, parts steep
Features:	River crossing, reindeer

From Rostahytta head south across the suspension bridge over Rostaela. Proceed uphill between Aslakvarri and Sikkalandjna and then wind through a chain of mountain tarns. Continue to climb

159

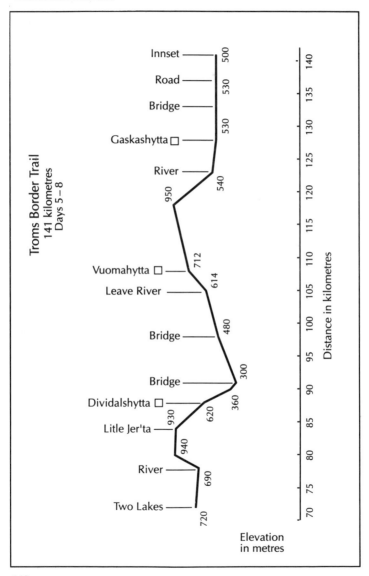

Troms Border Trail
141 kilometres
Days 5 – 8

Innset — 500
Road — 530
Bridge — 530
Gaskashytta ☐ — 530
River — 540
950
712
Vuomahytta ☐ — 614
Leave River — 614
480
Bridge — 300
Bridge — 300
Dividalshytta ☐ — 360
620
930
Litle Jer'ta — 940
River — 690
Two Lakes — 720

Distance in kilometres

140 135 130 125 120 115 110 105 100 95 90 85 80 75 70

Elevation
in metres

uphill more gradually now, and pass the northern shores of Lakes 948 and 946. You may have to remove your boots for a river crossing just past the lakes. All told, you will need 3 hours to reach the day's high point at just over 1000 metres. From there drop down to the boundary of Øvre Dividal National Park. A steep rocky descent follows; then grass greets you again. The two huts at Dærtahytta, another 20 minutes away, can be seen in the distance (U/20).

DÆRTAHYTTA (720m) to DIVIDALSHYTTA (620m) via HIGH POINT (940m)
7 hours, 24 kilometres

Elevation:	Rolling, parts steep
Features:	River crossing

From the hut follow the stream south, taking care not to take the trail west to Dividalen. Circle west of Harvesbak'ti above the river valley and after about one hour pass just south of Lake 875. For the first 2 hours you can look back and see Dærtahytta. Continue along many ups and downs, finally leaving the lake behind. After 3 hours walk between the two large lakes at about 725 metres toward the east side of stor Namna and circle around it. Now you are faced with a major river crossing over the wide Skaktardalen. If the water is low and you are lucky, stepping from stone to stone can lead you across. If the water is high take care and if possible use a walking stick for support. After crossing, climb steeply for one hour above the river and past the east side of Jer'ta to a high point of 940 metres. Descend the hillside below Litle Jer'ta.

On my visit here we saw a hillside vibrating with thousands of reindeer. Although a bit curious about us, most of them ran away. Reindeer may graze between 1 May and 15 September. These semi-domesticated herds should be left alone; do not approach them.

Proceed around Jer'ta to east and Litle Jer'ta to the west and then look south into the valley. Finally, after what seems an interminable number of ledges, you spot the huts below, just inside the trees. Climb very steeply down the slope and in a few minutes enter the trees. It is 10 minutes more along to the two huts at Dividalshytta (U/20), overlooking the Dividal valley.

DIVIDALSHYTTA (620m) to VUOMAHYTTA (712m)
6 hours, 20 kilometres

Elevation: Moderate, rolling

Leave the hut on a moderate downhill into the trees. Thirty minutes brings you to the river; walk along its banks for 30 minutes more in a fine birch forest. Parts of the track are overgrown. You come to a sign pointing west to Vuomahytta; turn here and cross the river on the suspension bridge. Proceed westward along the river's true right rarely out of earshot of the river. You now walk up and down in and out of bog for the next 4 hours. The day's halfway point is marked by a bridge over the river on the south-west slops of Nav'sti. The footing varies: going from firm trail to planks across bog to mud. Wild flowers of every colour imaginable line the route. You can follow your progress by first looking for Nav'sti to the south, then the river with the bridge over it and finally Blåfjellet to the south. At the west end of Blåfjellet turn south at a small pond, and then gain about 150 metres up over a knoll. Passing two small lakes, you surprisingly find yourself just a few minutes from the huts. Vuomahytta (U/20) is situated in a lovely alpine basin on the north shore of Vuomajav'ri. Snow capped peaks line Anjavassdalen to the north.

VUOMAHYTTA (712m) to GASKASHYTTA (530m) via HIGH POINT (950m)
6 hours, 20 kilometres

Elevation: Gradual

From the hut nestled between the peaks, head east. You will rise gradually for 3 hours until you reach the day's high point at 950 metres. The ground, at first soft and green, becomes rocky as you pass below several peaks. After one hour go by the end of the first chain of lakes, and pass the national park exit marker. A chain of cairns marks the path over the rocky terrain to the horizon ahead. The large distance between markers may make them hard to follow in poor weather. Some of the finest mountain scenery greets you as you continue east between Gai'bagai'si (1310m) and Doaresbak'ti (1152m). As you descend south-west into the verdant river valley wild whirled peaks hail you to the north-west. A one hour gradual descent follows to join the river valley. Descend the river valley where steep cliffs drop into the river. After an hour you enter the trees below the lovely green Gaskasvarri. Walk over the bridge and continue 5 minutes to Gaskashytta (U/10).

GASKASHYTTA (530m) to INNSET (500m)
4 hours 30 minutes, 14 kilometres

Elevation:	Almost level
Features:	Bus (limited), taxi service

From Gaskashytta follow the path through trees east and in 10 minutes cross the river on the bridge. Head toward the lake for $1/2$ kilometre and then veer east again. For the next 2 hours you slog around trees through mud; this can be very slow going. After 45 minutes move to the lake shore, for although this is rocky, it is less muddy and slippery. At the end of the lake proceed upstream on the river's true left another 15 minutes to the bridge. Cross over the bridge and on the other side the trail improves. After 30 minutes you see the first of several summer homes and 30 minutes more brings you to a road. Another hour on the road delivers you to Innset, a small summer community. Supplies are not available here; you can call to Sætermoen for a taxi. Or you may have planned to meet the weekly shopping bus to Sætermoen. You are in civilization at last. I hope you agree that you have encountered some of Norway's finest mountain scenery.

ALTERNATIVE ROUTES
From Innset your route can be extended south along the Nordkalottruta into Sweden to Lappjordhytta and to Bjørnfjell, connecting with the railway between Narvik and Sweden. If travelling from west to east you may wish to walk from Gåldahytta into Finland to Treriksrøysa and on to Kilpisjärvi. If you are full of energy continue along the Nordkalottruta into Finland.

CHAPTER 13:
The Far North

FINNMARKSVIDDA

Remember, the music is not in the piano

Clement Mok

On the northernmost edge of Europe the huge geographic area of Arctic Norway's Finnmark, including its mountain plateau Finnmarksvidda, covers close to 48,000 square kilometres or 15% of Norway's land area. Its 75,000 people, approximately half of whom are native reindeer-herding Sami or Lapps, comprise only 2% of the country's population. Due to the Gulf Stream the climate is surprisingly mild. Summer temperatures hover around 20° C, although they can rise to 25° to 30° C. Harbours remain ice free all year round. From the middle of May to the end of July the Midnight Sun shines. Some summers, this part of Norway boasts some of the finest weather of all of northern Europe.

The majority of the world's Sami, better known as Lapps, live on or near this mountain plateau. Their settlements stretch from Russia through the northern parts of Finland, Sweden and Norway. Kautokeino, near the Finnish border, is the Sami centre for culture, education and research. Karasjok is another well-known Sami settlement. You'll find Norwegian, Finnish and Sami spoken.

If this is your first visit to Finnmark, there are several sights to visit. Nordkapp 71° 10' 21" (North Cape) at the very top of Europe, is easily accessed from Honningsvåg. The 307-metre high cliff above the ocean makes a strong impression during the Midnight Sun, or even during its frequent fog. In 1992 over 200,000 people visited Nordkapp. The rock carvings at the Alta Museum, included on UNESCO's World Heritage List, are 2500-6500 years old. Guided museum tours are given in several languages. This impressive museum with its lovely grounds won the Best European Museum of the Year award in 1993.

There are over 60,000 lakes and several thousand kilometres of streams and rivers in Finnmark. Visitors encounter a variety of landscape from mountains to valleys to an immense indented coastline. The undulating mountain plateau of Finnmarksvidda, at an average height of 300 to 400 metres, has a rolling terrain dotted with splendid fishing lakes. Interspersed with birch forests and brushwood, its largely open area supports a floor of heather turf.

If you are skilled with map and compass and wish to use your tent Finnmarksvidda has unlimited possibilities. If looking for a bit more comfort the plateau is crossed by a few cairned routes linking up mountain lodges or *fjellstuer*. Walking along this plateau during the summer months is for the most part easy, although some complications may arise in marshy areas and on river crossings. On my walk here the route was well marked and rivers shallow enough for safe crossings. Mosquitoes, at their peak in late July, provided the main annoyance. In September the snow squalls of autumn will greet you. Lodges are open all year, although skiing the route in winter is a more serious undertaking than walking in the summer months.

The Lapp mountain lodges (*fjellstuer*) (see Appendix D), run by the state of Norway, are clean and well appointed, and provide pots and pans, gas rings and bedding. Only a few very basic provisions are on sale. If you intend to do your own cooking, you should bring along all your food. If you want to be served meals you must call ahead for a reservation. Rooms are simple, with several bunk beds. Like the huts in the southern part of the country, you need only a sheet sleeping bag. Though some publications recommend rubber boots, I found them unnecessary. The only extra equipment you'll need is mosquito netting for your head and strong repellent. Unmanned lodges marked on some maps are now closed.

MAPS
The old M711 1:50 000 maps are out of date and do not show several of the new trails. You can ask the guardian at the huts to outline the day's route for you.

BERRY PICKING IN FINNMARK
Cloudberries flourish throughout Finnmark. You will find them a rare treat. Growing in yellow bunches close to the ground, they turn

orange when ripe. Visitors to Finnmark may freely pick and eat cloudberries on the spot only, but may not carry them away. No such restrictions apply to the picking of other wild berries or mushrooms. Residents of Finnmark may take away any amount of any type of berries they pick.

TRANSPORT

Getting to Finnmark becomes part of the adventure, but you have to have plenty of both time and money. Several interesting transport options are available. You can fly to Alta, Hammerfest or Lakselv, and a bus will take you to the start of your walking tour at Karasjok. Or you might prefer the famous Coastal Express, Hurtigruten, which serves many of the northern coastal communities; good ferry and bus routes will then connect you with your tour. Hurtigruten must be reserved long in advance from the Bergen Line. From Oslo, with connections in Trondheim, you can take either the day and/or night trains to Bodø/Fauske, a journey of 18 hours. Bodø, the gateway to the North and the Lofoten Islands, celebrates the Midnight Sun from 2 June to 10 July. Join up with the coastal express or connect with the bus to the farther northern cities. Except for flying any travel option requires several days.

Route 20: FINNMARKSVIDDA

Distance:	59 kilometres
Time:	4-5 days
Rating:	Easy
Maps:	1934 II Iešjav'ri, 1934 III Suoluvuobmi, 1934 IV Gargia
	2033 IV Iešjåkka, 2034 III Stiipanav'ži
Start Altitude:	Assebak'ti, 150 metres
Highest Point:	Above Jotkajav'ri, 510 metres
Base:	Alta/Karasjok

ASSEBAK'TI (150m) to RAVNASTUA (360m) via HIGH POINT (400m)
4 hours, 15 kilometres

Terrain:	Almost level
Features:	Boat, bus, taxi

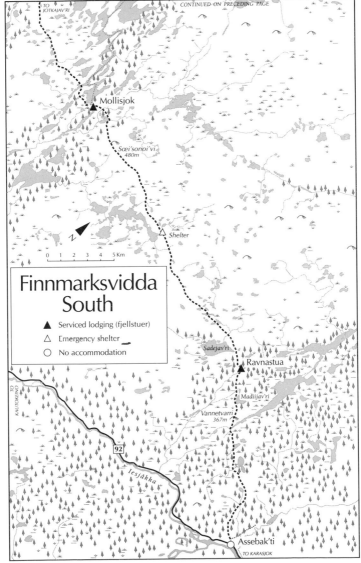

CONTINUED ON PRECEDING PAGE

TO
JOTKAJAV'RI

▲ Mollisjok

Sœi'sonpi'vi
480m

△ Shelter

0 1 2 3 4 5 Km

Finnmarksvidda South

▲ Serviced lodging (fjellstuer)

△ Emergency shelter

○ No accommodation

Sadejav'ri

▲ Ravnastua

Madiijav'ri

Vannetvarri
367m

TO
KAUTOKEINO

92

Iesjåkka

○ Assebak'ti

TO KARASJOK

167

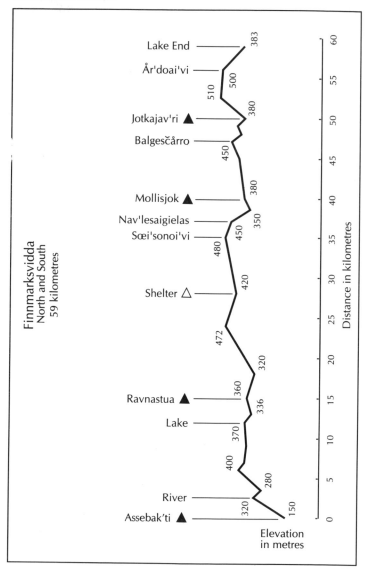

Finnmarksvidda
North and South
59 kilometres

Distance in kilometres

Elevation
in metres

Lake End — 383
År'doai'vi — 500
510
Jotkajav'ri ▲ — 380
Balgesčårro — 450
380
Mollisjok ▲ — 380
Nav'lesaigielas — 350
Sœi'sonoi'vi — 450
480
Shelter △ — 420
472
320
Ravnastua ▲ — 360
Lake — 336
370
400
280
River — 320
Assebak'ti ▲ — 150

From the Sami community of Karasjok take road 92 east 13 kilometres to the old farm Assebak'ti. You may wish to check with the tourist office about hiring a boat for the one hour river ride. There is also bus or taxi service down the road. After arriving at the far end pick up the old cart track across the road from the boat dock for an easy walk to Ravnastua. Initially you pass through a birch and pine forest. The track is easy to follow; an occasional red T reassures you that you are on the right path. You'll cross numerous easy streams and after one hour you'll wade across your first river. Ten minutes later you cross your next stream. After 2 hours in the trees you'll reach the day's high point at 400 metres. There are good views to the snow-capped Gaissene mountains in the north-east. After the high point you'll drop down again into the trees, crossing the flats near a couple of lake outlets. You then pass near the hill Vannetvarri (367m). After 4 hours you'll reach Ravnastua (F/22) a set of red painted buildings with a fine lake for swimming. The *fjellstue* was burnt down in 1944 by retreating German troops. The bunkhouse was rebuilt in 1947, and the main house was reconstructed in 1991.

RAVNASTUA (360m) to MOLLISJOK (380m) via HIGH POINT (480m)
7 hours, 25 kilometres

Terrain:	Almost level
Features:	Shelter

This is rather a long day, but not at all taxing. Leaving Ravnastua you head east past numerous lakes, wandering up and down, gaining only 100 metres in elevation for the first half of the day. At the halfway point you'll find an old *ödestue* or emergency shelter (U/8). It is always open and has bunk beds but no provisions or cooking facilities. Eventually you reach a high point at Sœi'sonoi'vi (480m) with good views of the expansive Finnmarksvidda continuing throughout the rest of the day. About one kilometre past Nav'lesaigielas you'll have to cross the wide river, no doubt getting your feet wet. It is about 3 kilometres more to the night's lodging at Mollisjok (F/24, sauna). If you are not too early in the season you'll see some of the famous low-growing orange cloudberries.

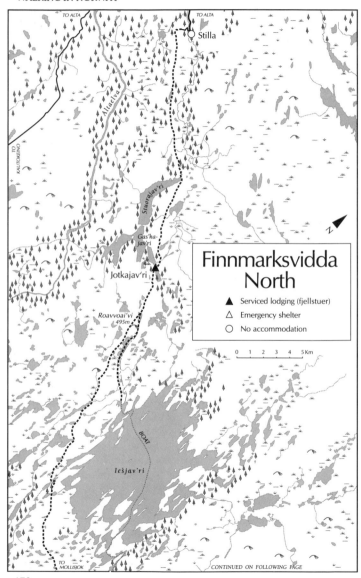

Finnmarksvidda North

▲ Serviced lodging (fjellstuer)

△ Emergency shelter

○ No accommodation

0 1 2 3 4 5 Km

TO ALTA

TO ALTA

Stilla

Altaelva

TO KAUTOKEINO

Stuorgjav'ri

Gas'ka-jav'ri

Jotkajav'ri

Roavvoai'vi
495m

BOAT

Iešjav'ri

TO MOLLISJOK

CONTINUED ON FOLLOWING PAGE

170

MOLLISJOK (380m) via boat to BOAT LANDING (400m) to JOTKAJAV'RI (380m)
3 hours, 10 kilometres (with boat)
10 hours, 35 kilometres (without boat)

Terrain:	Almost level
Features:	Boat or air option

If the weather is calm you may choose to shorten your day by taking the boat across the huge Lake Iešjav'ri. If you do you will ride across parts of the lake, stop in several spots, walk a short section of land and pick up the boat on the other side. I recommend you call ahead to tell the boatman at Mollisjok when you will want to use the boat. He will show you the boat stops on your map. Taking a plane may be an option as well, especially if windy weather grounds the boat.

From the boat stop head north-west to Roavvejav'ri, walking up its eastern shore. Your route passes south-west of the old path from the lake indicated on the map. The old path leaves from the northern edge of Lake 391. Meet the old track just north of the third of three lakes that dot the lake's northern shore. The trail from Mollisjok remains to your west.

If you decide to walk the whole way you will wish to inquire at Mollisjok about the new track. Find the old track on the map, as the new track starts about one kilometre south-south-west of the old one, north of the winter markings. The old *fjellstue* (*ödestue*) indicated on the map is now torn down. From the site of the old shelter your route heads north remaining on the west of the lake, undulating between 400 and 500 metres. Two kilometres north-west of Roavvoai'vi (495m) you join the northern track coming from the lake at Balgesčårro, and then it is only 5 kilometres to Jotkajav'ri (F/ 30).

JOTKAJAV'RI (380m) to LAKE END (383m) via HIGH POINT (510m)
3 hours, 9 kilometres

Terrain:	Almost level, parts moderate

From your stop at Jotkajav'ri you can call a taxi to meet you at several points along the track. Ask the guardian to help you locate

Finnmarksvidda

a convenient pick-up point, as there are no telephones at the far end. The many new roads in this section do not appear on the old 1:50 000 maps. Though not obvious from the older maps, taxis can now drive as far as the northern end of Stuorajav'ri, or can get to the western side of the peninsula that crosses the lake about 2 kilometres north-west of the *fjellstue*.

From Jotkajav'ri follow the road 30 minutes north up the hill to the high point at 510 metres. Now head north-west to the ridge above the lake where you amble along for 2 hours until you reach the lake's northern end. If you are heading all the way to Stilla you've still got 12 kilometres to go from here. Or you can pick up a taxi to Tverrelvdalen (no phone) and then a bus to Alta.

APPENDICES

APPENDIX A: Summary Table of Routes

Route 1: Hardangervidda West
Fossli (670m)

1h	Skissete (980m)
45min	High Point (1140m)
1h	Berdstø (914m)
45min	Below Fljotdals (1200m)
45min	River Fljotdal (980m)
40min	Hedlo (945m)
1h	Rjoto (900m)
1h	High Point (1100m)
30min	Hadlaskard (1000m)
1h 30min	Viersdalen (1140m)
1h 15min	Solnuten (1300m)
45min	Lake (1268m)
10min	Top (1350m)
10min	Torehytta (1340m)
20min	High Point (1430m)
40min	Above Lake (1184m)
1h 30min	Batadalen (1200m)
30min	Turnoff to Hadlaskard (1194m)
1h	Helnaberg (1180m)
1h	Lona (1129m)
20min	Stavali 1024m)
1h	Grøndulen (1000m)
40min	Vierdalen (1100m)
1h 20min	River Kinso (600m)
1h	Kraftverk (200m)
1h	Kinsarvik (10m)

Route 2: Hardangervidda Central
Dyranut (1240m)

1h	Nybu (1100m)
2h	Hellehalsen (1260m)
2h	Below Trondavndnatane (1280m)
1h	Sandhaug (1252m)
1h	Eriksbalen (1260m)
2h 30min	Isthmus (1212m)
1h 30min	Trondsbu (1220m)
2h	Rauhellern (1220m)

1h	High Point (1300m)
2h 30min	Boat Dock - Halne (1135m)
40min	High Point (1260m)
40min	Krækkja (1161m)
1h 15min	Below Langhaugen (1300m)
2h 45min	Kjeldebu (1060m)
30min	Langetjørndalen (1100m)
2h	Below Dyranutane (1300m)
30min	Dyranut (1240m)

Route 3: Aurlandsdalen
Finse (1222m)

2h 30min	Klemsbu (1610m)
30min	Sankt Pål (1694m)
1h	Above East Omnsvatnet (1380m)
1h	Geitrygghytta (1229m)
1h 45min	High Point (1380m)
1h 15min	Steinbergdalen (1070m)
1h 30min	High Point (1250m)
1h 30min	Grønestøl (1000m)
1h	Østerbø (820m)
1h	To Holmen (780m)
1h	Bjørnstigen (1000m)
30min	Join main track (720m)
20min	To Vetlahelvete (700m)
50min	To Bridge (650m)
20min	Waterfall (610m)
10min	Sinjarheim (700m)
1h 30min	Car park (131m)
20min	Vassbygdi/Kiosk (94m)

Route 4: Jotunheimen East to West
Gjendesheim (995m)

2h	High Point (1743m)
5min	Besseggen (1700m to 1300m)
40min	Bessvatnet (1373m)
1h	High Point (1518m)
2h 15min	Memurubu (1008m)
1h	High Point (1400m)
1h	Russvatnet - South (1175m)

45min	Russvatnet - North (1175m)
1h 15min	High Point (1685m)
2h	Glitterheim (1384m)
3h 30min	Glittertind (2464m)
3h 30min	Spiterstulen (1106m)
3h 30min	Kyrkjeglupen (1500m)
1h 30min	Leirvassbu (1400m)
3h 45min	Turnoff to Olavsbu (1000m)
1h 45min	Skogadalsbøen (843m)
1h 30min	High Point (1200m)
1h 15min	Fleskedalen (972m)
1h 15min	Vettismorki (683m)
1h	Vetti (317m)
1h 15min	Road End - Hjelle (260m)

Route 5: Jotunheimen South
Gjendesheim (995m)

2h	High Point (1743m)
5min	Besseggen (1700m to 1300m)
40min	Bessvatnet (1373m)
1h	High Point (1518m)
2h 15min	Memurubu (1008m)
2h	Grunnevatnet (1443m)
1h 30min	To Leirvassbu (1480m)
45min	Lake (984m)
1h	Gjendebu (990m)
2h	To Fondsbu (1440m)
3h	Olavsbu (1440m)
45min	Rauddalsvatnet West (1313m)
15min	Turnoff to Skogadalsbøen (1313m)
30min	Rauddalsvatnet East (1313m)
1h 30min	Lake (1265m)
1h 20min	To Leirvassbu (1000m)
1h 20min	To Krossbu (820)
20min	Skogadalsbøen (843m)
15min	To Fannaråkhytta (820m)
1h 30min	Jervatnet (1395m)
30min	To Turtagrø (1500m)
1h 30min	Fannaråknosi (1990m)
30min	Fannaråkhytta (2068m)
2h	To Skogadalsbøen (1200m)
1h	Turtagrø (884m)

Route 6: Jotunheimen West
Sognefjellhytta (1411m)

2h	Glacier (1500m)
2h 30min	Fannaråknosi (1990m)
30min	Fannaråkhytta (2068m)
30min	Fannaråknosi (1990m)
1h 30min	Lake (1400m)
1h 30min	Skogadalsbøen (843m)
2h	To Olavsbu (1000m)
4h	Leirvassbu (1400m)
20min	Turnoff to glacier (1400m)
40min	Glacier (1500m)
2h	Top (1900m)
3h	Krossbu (1267m)

Route 7: Rondane Traverse
Hjerkinn (950m)

45min	Hageseter (916m)
2h	High Point (1340m)
40min	Above Tverråi (1200m)
20min	Tverråi (1100m)
45min	Grimsdalshytta (994m)
2h	High Point (1300m)
1h	Haverdalsåi (980m)
2h	High Point (1300m)
45min	Dørålseter (1040m)
2h	Bergedalen (1233m)
1h	Rondvatnet (1167m)
0	by boat toRondvassbu (1165m)
2h 30min	Illmanndalen West (1280m)
1h	Illmanndalen East (1280m)
30min	Bjørnhollia (914m)
30min	High Point (914m)
45min	Marsh (990m)
45min	Straumbu (740m)

Route 8: Rondane Tops
Rondvassbu (1165m)

1h	Rondholet (1470m)
1h 30min	Vinjeronden (2044m)
1h 30min	Rondslottet (2178m)
1h 30min	Turnoff to Dørålseter (1240m)
1h	Turnoff to Høgronden

	(1080m)
1h 30min	Bjørnhollia (914m)
1h 45min	Turnoff to Høgronden
	(1080m)
3h	Høgronden (2115m)
1h	Lake (1460m)
3h 30min	Dørålseter (1040m)
2h 15min	Bergedalen (1233m)
45min	Rondvatnet (1165m)
	on foot to
45min	Ridge (1647m)
30min	To Veslesmeden (1540m)
45min	Top of ridge (1871m)
15min	Below top (1900m)
30min	Veslesmeden (2015m)
10min	Below top (1900m)
10min	End of ridge (1871m)
25min	Turnoff to Rondvassbu
	(1540m)
45min	Rondvassbu (1165m)

Route 9: Rondane Circle
Rondvassbu (1165m)

1h 30min	Illmanndalen West (1280m)
30min	Illmanndalen East (1280m)
2h	Bjørnhollia (914m)
1h 30min	Turnoff to Høgronden
	(1080m)
2h	High Point (1418m)
45min	Turnoff to Rondvassbu
	(1320m)
1h	Begedalen (1200m)
1h 45min	Døralseter (1040m)
1h 15min	Bergedalen (1200m)
45min	Lakes (1233m)
1h	Rondvatnet (1167m)
0	by boat to Rondvassbu
	(1165m)

Route 10: Alvdal Vestfjell (Low Route)
Flatseter (800m)

1h	High Route turnoff (940m)
2h	Breisjøseter (951m)
1h	To Straumbu (1200m)
	(turnoff below Breisjøkinn)
1h 30min	Lake (1370m)

30min	Gravskardet (1482m)
45min	Turnoff to Flatseter (1280m)
45min	Indre Kampen (1180m)
30min	Straumbu (740m)

Route 11: Alvdal Vestfjell (High Route)
Flatseter (800m)

1h 15min	Low Route turnoff (940m)
45min	Track to Breisjøseter (1100m)
1h	First Top, Sølnkletten
	(1690m)
25min	Low Point (1579m)
35min	Second Top, Sølnkletten
	(1827m)
30min	Turnoff to Breisjøseter
	(1200m)
30min	Breisjøseter (951m)
1h	To Straumbu (1200m)
1h 30min	Lake (1370m)
30min	Gravskardet (1482m)
45min	Turnoff to Flatseter (1280m)
45min	Indre Kampen (1180m)
30min	Straumbu (740m)
2h	Bjørnhollia (914m)

Route 12: Tafjord
Tunga (800m)

3h	Pyttbua (1156m)
1h 15min	End Lake (1170m)
1h 15min	Top (1544m)
1h 15min	To Vakkerstøylen (1180m)
2h 15min	Reindalseter (710m)
1h	Waterfall (460m)
1h	Parking (450m)

Route 13: Dovre Mountains
Kongsvoll (890m)

40min	National Park Entrance
	(1120m)
1h 20min	Footbridge (1160m)
1h 15min	Lake (1289m)
1h	Reinheim (1340m)
40min	To Snøheim (1400m)
1h 50min	To Snøheim (1880m)
1h	Snøhetta (2286m)
1h 15min	End of snow (1800m)

2h	Åmotdalshytta (1310m)
2h	To Jenstad (1380m)
1h 15min	Loennechenbua (1351m)
2h	Flatskirådalen (1270m)
1h 45min	Turnoff to Jenstad (780m)
20min	Gammelseter (810m)
2h	Gjøra (205m)

Route 14: Trollheimen Traverse
Gjevilvasshytta (700m)

2h	High Point (1000m)
1h	River Minilla (900m)
1h 30min	High Point (1060m)
1h 30min	Jøldalshytta (720m)
1h 30min	Langfjellet (1240m)
1h 45min	Lakes (1160m)
1h 45min	Trollhetta 1 (1523m)
15min	Pass (1460m)
30min	Trollhetta 2 (1596m)
15min	Pass (1480m)
45min	Trollhetta 3 (1616m)
1h 30min	Marsh (700m)
45min	Trollheimshytta (540m)
5h	High Point (973m)
20min	Shelter (830m)
2h 40min	Kårvatn (210m)
30min	Turnoff (210m)
45min	Farm (600m)
2h 15min	Bjøråskardet (1180m)
1h 30min	Innerdalen (400m)
1h 30min	Lake (729m)
2h 30min	High Point (1000m)
2h	Fale (110m)

Route 15: Trollheimen Circle
Gjevilvasshytta (700m)

2h	High Point (1000m)
1h	River Minilla (900m)
1h 30min	High Point (1060m)
1h 30min	Jøldalshytta (720m)
30min	Turnoff to Geithetta (700m)
3h 30min	Below Geithetta (1250m)
2h	Trollheimshytta (540m)
2h 30min	Skallen (1226m)
45min	Mellom (1194m)
45min	Fossådalsvatnet (1188m)

1h	Pass (1320m)
1h	Kamtjørnin (1147m)
2h	Gjevilvasshytta (700m)

Route 16: Sylene
Stugudal (610m)

1h	Vektarhaugen (780m)
3h 30min	Boat Shed (720m)
30min	Nedalshytta (780m)
3h 15min	High Point (1143m)
15min	Ekorrdøren (Shelter 1135m)
45min	High Point (1380m)
2h 30min	Sylstationen (1043m)
30min	High Point (1150m)
2h 30min	Border (1100m)
2h 30min	Bridge at Lake (700m)
30min	Storerikvollen (760m)
1h 30min	Bridge at Lake (700m)
30min	Border (800m)
30min	Shelter (880m)
2h 30min	Blåhammaren (1085m)
1h 15min	Shelter (880m)
1h 15min	Trail Junction (500m)
1h 30min	High Point (760m)
1h	Storlien (590m)

Route 17: Femundsmarka
Røoset (660m)

20min	National Park Boundary (700m)
40min	Røvollen (709m)
30min	Nedre Roasten (720m)
1h 15min	Lakes (776m)
1h 30min	Falkfangarhøgda (960m)
1h 30min	Svukuriset (819m)
1h	High Point (850m)
2h	Elgå (662m)

Route 18: Mountains of Narvik
Katterat (400m)

45min	Hunddalstoppen (700m)
45min	Langryggen (780m)
1h	Road (635m)
1h	Hunddalshytta (700m)
1h 15min	High Point (900m)
1h 45min	Shelter (859m)

3h	Čunojávri (709m)
1h 15min	High Point (731m)
1h 45min	Road (690m)
1h 30min	Turnoff to Hut (602m)
30min	Lossihytta (700m)
1h 15min	East End Lossivatnet (700m)
2h 15min	Rienatvággi (1116m)
2h	Crossing (800m)
1h 45min	Lake 805 (805m)
45min	Hunddalshytta (700m)
3h	Katterat (400m)

Route 19: Troms Border Trail
Near Border - Galgujav'ri (520m)

1h	Base of Hill (680m)
1h	High Point (930m)
45min	Lakes (840m)
1h 15min	Gåldahytta (527m)
45min	Lake Outlet (500m)
1h	Below Gåldahaugen (647m)
2h 15min	Gappohytta (706m)
45min	Border (760m)
1h 15min	Border (900m)
1h	High Point (1001m)
3h	Rostahytta (463m)
1h	Lake (746m)
2h 45min	Top (1000m)
15min	National Park (950m)
1h 30min	Dærtahytta (720m)
90min	River Crossing (750m)
90min	Between Two Lakes (720m)
2h	River Crossing (690m)
1h	Top (940m)
1h 15min	Below Litle Jer'ta (930m)
1h 15min	Dividalshytta (620m)
30min	River (360m)
30min	Bridge (300m)
2h	Second Bridge (480m)
2h	Leave River (614m)
1h	Vuomahytta (712m)
3h	High Point (950m)
1h 30min	River (540m)
1h 30min	Gaskashytta (530m)
2h 30min	Bridge (500m)
1h	Road - Lake End (500m)
1h	Innset (500m)

Route 20: Finnmarksvidda
Assebak'ti (150m)

10min	Turnoff (200m)
50min	River 1 (320m)
1h	High Point (400m)
40min	Lake Outlet (370m)
10min	Lake Outlet 2 (360m)
10min	Madiijav'ri (336m)
1h	Ravnastua (360m)
45min	First Stream (320m)
1h 30min	High Point (472m)
1h 15min	Shelter (420m)
2h	Sœi'sonoi'vi (480m)
30min	Nav'lesaigielas (450m)
45min	River Crossing (350m)
15min	Mollisjok (380m)
	by boat to
	Boat Landing
1h 15min	Join Old Track (410m)
45min	Balgesčårro (450m)
15min	Creek (400m)
15min	Top (420m)
30min	Jotkajav'ri (380m)
20min	Top (510m)
30min	År'doai'vi (500m)
2h 10min	End of Lake (383m)

APPENDIX B: Mountain Accommodation

Mountain huts run by the DNT or associated touring organizations are designated as full-service (B), self-service (SS), or unstaffed (U). The level of service (e.g. B) is indicated first and the number of beds available noted next (e.g. B/25). Private mountain accommodation and the number of beds available are indicated by P followed by the number of beds (e.g. P/25). Huts in the Sylene owned by the Swedish touring association are marked as SNT followed by the number of beds (e.g. SNT/45). Staffed lodging in Finnmark (both full service and self-service) is indicated by F followed by the number of beds (e.g. F/12).

B: Full-service staffed hut
SS: Self-service hut
U: Unstaffed hut
P: Private staffed lodging (full-service private mountain hut or other accommodation in villages or towns)
F: Full-service and self-serviced lodging in Finnmark
H: Hotels in cities and larger towns

Alvdal: (Alvdal Vestfjell) H, railway station, bus, taxi, limited provisions
Alvundeid: (Trollheimen) bus, taxi, no provisions
Bergen: H, Norway's second largest city, railway station, coastal express, bus, taxi, airport, full provisions
Bjoreidalshytta: (Hardangervidda) 1140m, P/38
Bjorli: (Tafjord) H, railway station, bus, taxi, limited provisions
Bjørnhollia: (Jotunheimen) 914m, B/90
Blåhammaren: (Sylene) 1085m, SNT/28, limited provisions, Sweden's highest mountain hut
Bodø: H, railway station, bus, taxi, airport, coastal express, full provisions
Breisjøseter: (Alvdal Vestfjell) 951m, P/48
Čunojávri: (Mountains of Narvik) 709m, U/13
Dividalshytta: (Troms Border Trail) 620m, U/20
Dombås: H, railway station, bus, full provisions

Dyranut: (Hardangervidda) 1240m, P/35, bus

Dærtahytta: (Troms Border Trail) 720m, U/20

Dørålseter, Upper: (Rondane) 1040m, P/100

Enafors: (Sylene) 490m, H, railway station, bus, taxi, limited provisions

Fale: (Trollheimen) 110m, P, bus

Fannaråkhytta: (Jotunheimen) 2068m, B/35, Norway's highest mountain hut

Finse: (Aurlandsdalen) 1222m, H, limited provisions, railway station

Finsehytta: (Aurlandsdalen) 1222m, B/150, railway station

Flatseter: (Alvdal Vestfjell) 800m, P/9

Fondsbu: (Jotunheimen) 1065m, B/92, boat

Fossli: (Hardangervidda) 670m, H

Frankseter: (Alvdal Vestfjell) 800m, P/19

Gammelseter: (Dovre) 810m, SS/22

Gappohytta: (Troms Border Trail) 706m, U/20

Gaskashytta: (Troms Border Trail) 530m, U/20

Geiterygghytta: (Aurlandsdalen) 1229m, B/82, bus

Gjendebu: (Jotunheimen) 990m, B/115, boat

Gjendesheim: (Jotunheimen) 995m, B/143, bus, boat

Gjevilvasshytta: (Trollheimen) 700m, B/54, taxi

Gjøra: (Dovre) 205m, P, bus

Glitterheim: (Jotunheimen) 1384m, B/130

Grimsdalshytta: (Rondane) 994m, B/54

Gåldahytta: (Troms Border Trail) 527m, U/20

Hadlaskard: (Hardangervidda) 1000m, SS/34

Hageseter: (Rondane) 916m, P/70

Halne: (Hardangervidda) 1135m, P/65

Hedlo: (Hardangervidda) 945m, P/50

Hjelle: (Jotunheimen) 260m, bus, taxi

Hjerkinn: (Rondane) 950m, P/88, railway station, bus

Hunddalshytta: (Mountains of Narvik) 700m, U/14

Innerdalshytta: (Trollheimen) 400m, P/50

Innset: (Troms Border Trail) P (very limited), bus (very limited), taxi, no provisions

Jotkajav'ri: (Finnmarksvidda) 380m, F/30

Juvvasshytta: (Jotunheimen) 1841m, P/75, Galdhøpiggen summit tours

Jøldalshytta: (Trollheimen) 720m, B/48
Kaldhusseter: (Tafjord) 600m, B/42
Kinsarvik: (Hardangervidda) 10m, H, ferry, bus, taxi, tourist
    office, limited provisions
Kjeldebu: (Hardangervidda) 1060m, SS/40
Kongsvoll: (Dovre) 890m, P/50
Krossbu: (Jotunheimen) 1267m, P/75
Krækkja: (Hardangervidda) 1161m, B/85
Kårvatn: (Trollheimen) 210m, SS/19
Leirvassbu: (Jotunheimen) 1400m, P/190, glacier tours
Liseth: (Hardangervidda) 750m, P/40
Litlos: (Hardangervidda) 1180m, B/52
Loennechenbua: (Dovre) 1351m, U/2
Lossihytta: (Mountains of Narvik) 700m, U/14
Memurubu: (Jotunheimen) 1008m, P/140, boat
Mollisjok: (Finnmarksvidda) 380m, F/24
Mysusæter: (Rondane) 900m, H, bus, taxi, limited provisions
Narvik: H, railway station with connections to Sweden, bus, taxi,
    airport (Narvik and Evenes), full provisions
Nedalshytta: (Sylene) 780m, B/54, boat
Olavsbu: (Jotunheimen) 1440m, SS/35
Oppdal: H, railway station, bus, taxi, full provisions
Oslo: H, Norway's largest city and capital, railway station with
    connections to Sweden and Central Europe, airport, bus, taxi,
    full provisions
Otta: H, railway station, bus, taxi, limited provisions, tourist
    office
Pyttbua: (Tafjord) 1156m, SS/55
Rauhellern: (Hardangervidda) 1220m, B/65
Ravnastua: (Finnmarksvidda) 360m, F/20
Reindalseter: (Tafjord) 710m, B/93
Reinheim: (Dovre) 1340m, SS/38
Renndølsetra: (Trollheimen) 400m, P/30
Rondvassbu: (Rondane) 1165m, B/128
Rostahytta: (Troms Border Trail) 463m, U/20
Røros: (Femundsmarka) H, railway station, bus, taxi, airport, full
    provisions
Røvollen: (Femundsmarka) 709m, SS/21

Sandhaug: (Hardangervidda) 1252m, B/80

Skogadalsbøen: (Jotunheimen) 843m, B/55

Sognefjellhytta: (Jotunheimen) 1411m, P/50

Spiterstulen: (Jotunheimen) 1106m, P/120, bus, cafeteria, Galdhøpiggen summit tours

Stadsbuøy: (Rondane) P/SS/22, 800m

Stavali: (Hardangervidda) 1024m, SS/36

Steinbergdalen: (Aurlandsdalen) 1070m, P/50

Storerikvollen: (Sylene) 760m, B/65, boat

Storlien: (Sylene) 590m, H, railway station, bus, taxi, limited provisions

Straumbu: (Rondane) 740m, P/30, bus (seasonal)

Stugudal: (Sylene) 610m, H, bus, limited provisions

Svukuriset: (Femundsmarka) 819m, B/43

Sylstationen: (Sylene) 1043m, SNT/90

Sætermoen: (Troms Border Trail) H, bus, taxi, limited provisions, tourist office

Torehytten: (Hardangervidda) 1340m, SS/22

Trollheimshytta: (Trollheimen) 540m, B/55

Tromsø: H, bus, taxi, airport, coastal steamer, full provisions

Trondheim: H, Norway's third largest city, railway station with connections to Norway and Sweden, airport, bus, taxi, coastal steamer, full provisions

Turtagrø: (Jotunheimen) 884m, P/80, bus, limited provisions

Vassbygdi: (Aurlandsdalen) 94m, bus

Vektarhaugen: (Sylene) 780m, SS/7

Vetti: (Jotunheimen) 317m, P/20

Vettismorki: (Jotunheimen) 683m, U/4

Viveli: (Hardangervidda) 880m, P/8 (no service in 1995)

Vuomahytta: (Troms Border Trail) 712m, U/20

Østerbø: (Aurlandsdalen) 820m, P/110

Øvre Årdal: (Jotunheimen) H, bus, ferry connections, limited provisions

Åmotdalshytta: (Dovre) 1310m, SS/30

Årdalstangen: (Jotunheimen) H, bus, ferry, limited provisions

APPENDIX C: Norwegian and Swedish Train Lines to Walking Routes

Route	Area	Train Lines	Train Stop/Other Transport Needed
1, 2	Hardangervidda	Oslo to Bergen (Bergen Line)	Geilo/bus
3	Aurlandsdalen (start)	Oslo to Bergen (Bergen Line)	Finse
3	Aurlandsdalen (end)	Flåm to Myrdal (Flåm Line) (connect from Bergen Line)	Flåm/bus
4, 5, 6	Jotunheimen	Oslo to Trondheim (Dovre Line)	Otta/bus
7	Rondane	Oslo to Trondheim (Dovre Line)	Hjerkinn
8, 9	Rondane	Oslo to Trondheim (Dovre Line)	Otta/taxi or bus
10, 11	Alvdal Vestfjell	Oslo to Trondheim (Røros Line)	Alvdal/taxi
12	Tafjord	Dombås to Åndalsnes (Romsdal Line) (connect from Dovre Line)	Bjorli/taxi
13	Dovre Mountains	Oslo to Trondheim (Dovre Line)	Kongsvoll
14, 15	Trollheimen	Oslo to Trondheim (Dovre Line)	Oppdal/taxi or bus
16	Sylene	Trondheim to Stockholm (Swedish Line)	Storlien/Enafors taxi or bus
17	Femundsmarka	Oslo to Trondheim (Røros Line)	Røros/bus and boat
18	Mountains of Narvik	Narvik to Stockholm (Ofot Line)	Katterat
19	Troms Border Trail	Trondheim to Bodø (Nordland Line)	Bodø/bus
20	Finnmarksvidda	Trondheim to Bodø (Nordland Line)	Bodø/bus

APPENDIX D: Helpful Addresses

Norwegian Mountain Touring Association:
Den Norske Turistforening: Boks 1963 Vika, N-0125, Oslo (22 83 25 50)
Street Address: Stortingsgt 28, Oslo

Associated Mountain Touring Association Offices:
Alta og Omegn Turlag: Boks 1129, 9501 Alta
Bergen Turlag: Tverrgt 4/6, 5017 Bergen (55 32 22 30)
Narvik og Omegn Turistforening: Boks 615, N-8501 Narvik (76 94 37 90)
(maps and keys at the Narvik Fire Station)
Trondhjems Turistforening: Munkegaten 64, 7011 Trondheim (73 52 38 08)
(maps, keys, and information)
Troms Turlag: Boks 284, 9001 Tromsø (77 68 51 75)
Street Address: Sjøgaten 17

Mountain Lodges in Finnmark:
Mollisjok: 9730 Karasjok (78 46 91 16)
Jotkajav'ri: 9500 Alta (98 43 45 54)
Ravnastua: 9730 Karasjok (98 80 06 88)

Tourist Offices:
Bergen Tourist Information: Bryggen 7, Bergen (55 32 14 80)
Finnmark Opplevelser: PO Box 1223, N-9501 Alta (78 43 55 59)

Narvik Tourist Office: Narvik Bus Station, Narvik (76 94 33 09)
Norway Information Centre: Rådhusplassen, Oslo (22 83 00 50)
Norway Tourist Office: Oslo Central Station, Oslo (22 17 11 24)
Sætermoan Tourist Office: Sætermoan (77 18 21 88)
Troms Reiser A/S: PO Box 1077, N-9001, Tromsø (77 61 00 00)
Trondheim Tourist Association: Munkegaten 19, Trondheim (73 92 94 06)

Map Sellers:
Olaf Norlis Bokhandel: Universitetsgata 20-24, Oslo
Tanum Libris: Karl Johans Gate 43, Oslo
Beyer Bok-Og Papirhandel: Strandgate 4, Bergen
Melvær Libris: Småstrandgaten 1, Bergen
Platou Sport: Småstrandgaten 8, Bergen
Bruns Libris: Kongensgate 10, 7011 Trondheim
Edward Stanford Ltd: 12-14 Long Acre, London WC2E 9LP
The Map Shop, 15 High Street, Upton-upon-Severn, Worcs. WR8 OHJ

APPENDIX E: Glossary of Norwegian Words

afternoon	*ettermiddag*	key	*nøkkel*
airport	*lufthavn*	lady	*dame*
airport bus	*flybussen*	lake, water	*vann*
beautiful	*vakker*	laundromat	*mynt-vaskeri*
bottom, i.e.,valley floor	*botn,*	lavatory	*W.C.*
	bunn, dalbunn	men	*menn*
breakfast	*frokost*	morning	*morgen*
bridge	*bru, bro*	mountain	*fjell*
caution	*forsiktig*	mountain path	*fjellsti*
closed	*stengt*	mountain peak	*toppen*
crown (coin)	*krone*	mountain plateau	*vidde*
danger	*fare*	night	*natt*
dinner	*middag*	No smoking	*Røking forbudt*
emergency shelter	*ødestue*	On Foot in	*Til Fots*
entrance	*inngang*	the Mountains	*i Fjellet*
excuse me	*unnskyld*	on the left	*til venstre*
exit	*utgang*	on the right	*til høyre*
foot	*fot*	peninsula	*halvøy*
gentlemen	*herrer*	please	*vær så snill*
good day	*god dag*	post office	*posthus*
good morning	*god morgen*	post office box	*postboks*
Have a good trip!		railway	*jernbane*
Bon voyage!	*God tur!*	railway station	*jernbanestasjon*
hello	*god dag*	rain	*regn*
High Peak (the)	*Galdhøpiggen*	restaurant	*restaurant*
Home of the Giants	*Jotunheimen*	sheet sleeping bag	*lakenpose*
Home of the Trolls	*Trollheimen*	Sparkling Peak	*Glittertind*
hostel	*vandrerhjem*	stop	*stopp*
hut	*hytte*	straight ahead	*rett frem*
hut (in Finnmark)	*fjellstue*	taxi	*drosje, taxi*
hut - full-service	*betjent hytte*	Thank you	*takk*
hut - self-service	*selvbetjent hytte*	today	*i dag*
hut - unstaffed	*ubetjent hytte*	toilet	*toalett*
hut or small cabin	*bu*	tomorrow	*i morgen*
inner valley	*Innerdalen*	tourist hut	*turisthytte*
keep out	*ingen adgang*	tourist office	*turistkontor*

train; railway	*tog, jernbane*	twenty	*tjue*
train station	*jernbanestasjon*	thirty	*tretti*
viewpoint	*utsiktspunkt*	forty	*førti*
Warning!	*Fare!*	fifty	*femti*
water	*vann, vatn*	sixty	*seksti*
women	*kvinner*	seventy	*sytti*
yes/no	*ja/nei*	eighty	*åtti*
You're welcome	*vær så god*	ninety	*nitti*
		one hundred	*et hundre*
one	*en*	two hundred	*to hundre*
two	*to*	one thousand	*et tusen*
three	*tre*		
four	*fire*	Monday	*mandag*
five	*fem*	Tuesday	*tirsdag*
six	*seks*	Wednesday	*onsdag*
seven	*syv, sju*	Thursday	*torsdag*
eight	*åtte*	Friday	*fredag*
nine	*ni*	Saturday	*lørdag*
ten	*ti*	Sunday	*søndag*

APPENDIX F: A Visit to the Romsdal

If walking in the Tafjord you should not miss a visit to the neighbouring Romsdal, without doubt Norway's most famous climbing area. Unfortunately, no overnight walking routes will guide you through this magnificent terrain. However, you can view these ragged peaks, sheer cliff walls and overhangs in several ways. The view from the train from Dombås to Åndalsnes is splendid and passes just below the cliff walls. The famous Trollvegen (the Troll's Wall) (1370m) rises 1000 metres from its base, and draws climbers from all over the world. The Romdalshorn (1554m) can also be seen from the train. The Åndalsnes tourist office, located next to the train station, can help you arrange day walking tours and climbs of some of the neighbouring cliffs.

From Åndalsnes a summer bus route connects Åndalsnes with Valldal, Geiranger and Ålesund, along the Trollstigen (the Troll's Path). The 56-kilometre Trollstigen, which took one hundred men 20 summers to build, reaches its apex at 850 metres above sea level. From a platform at Stigrøra you can view the mountain formations: Karitind, Dronningen (the Queen), Kongen (the King), the Bispen (the Bishop) as well as the road's 11 hairpin turns. From Valldal you can catch a bus to Tafjord and connect to the western end of Route 12 Tafjord.

The famous jagged peaks of Trolltindene on the eastern side of nearby Isterdalen constitute the most heralded and magnificent rock formations in Norway. Its pointed peaks purport to be the remains of mountain trolls turned to stone by the sun. Legends say that the trolls held a wedding feast, and celebrated so late that the sun came up, and the wedding party turned to stone. You'll see the entire wedding party: Trollgubben (the Troll), Trollkjerringa (the Troll Woman), the Bride, the Bridegroom and the Best Man.

APPENDIX G: Time in Oslo and Bergen

Norway's centre of commerce and lifeline to the sea, Oslo boasts a distinct international flavour. Large in area, it is home to only 500,000 people. The city is tourist friendly and easy to get about, whether on foot, bus or train. Parks, trees, museums, shopping, hiking and cross-country ski trails and panoramic views provide the visitor with many worthwhile activities.

Oslo's highlights are many; only a few will be mentioned here. Located around the vibrant compact central area are the Royal Palace, National Museum, National Theatre, City Hall and Resistance Museum. A short boat ride from the centre to the Bygdøy Peninsula and you'll find the Kon-Tiki, the Viking Ship Museum, the Norwegian Folk Museum and the Gol Stave Church. Holmenkollen Ski Jump and Museum, seen from many points in the city and a short train ride away, was built for the 1952 Olympics, and is not far from the Munch Museum. Frogner Park (Vigeland sculpture park), a 20-minute walk from the centre, is especially lovely in the evening. There really is nothing like it anywhere in the world. The life's work of Gustav Vigeland lines the park paths, and makes up the central monolithic structure. Be sure to visit it yourself, and form your own opinion on his over 200 sculptures.

Bergen, with 220,000 inhabitants on the country's south-west coast and at the foot of seven mountains, is another shipping centre with a strong cultural heart. Enclosed by the sea and fjords, this cosy and rainy city seems far away from the rest of Norway. Off the centre are the fish market and Fløybanen, a funicular to a lookout 326 metres above the sea. Also worth a visit are St. Mary's Church, the oldest building in Bergen, the King's Hall, Rosenkrantz Tower and Hanseatisk Museum. Bryggen, with its old wooden buildings, is considered a significant monument to medieval Europe. A short ride from the town centre brings you to Troldhaugen (Edvard Grieg's House) and the Fantoft Stave Church. Many cruise ships dock here in summertime, and in 1995 Bergen was Europe's largest cruise harbour.

NOTES

CICERONE GUIDES

Cicerone publish a wide range of reliable guides to walking and climbing worldwide

ITALY & SLOVENIA

ALTA VIA - High Level Walks in the Dolomites

THE CENTRAL APENNINES OF ITALY Walks, scrambles & Climbs

THE GRAND TOUR OF MONTE ROSA (inc Switzerland)

WALKS IN ITALY'S GRAN PARADISO

LONG DISTANCE WALKS IN THE GRAN PARADISO

ITALIAN ROCK - Rock Climbs in Northern Italy

VIA FERRATA - Scrambles in the Dolomites

WALKING IN THE DOLOMITES

WALKS IN THE JULIAN ALPS

MEDITERRANEAN COUNTRIES

THE ATLAS MOUNTAINS

CRETE: Off the beaten track

WALKING IN CYPRUS

THE MOUNTAINS OF GREECE

THE MOUNTAINS OF TURKEY

TREKS & CLIMBS IN WADI RUM, JORDAN

THE ALA DAG - Climbs & Treks (Turkey)

HIMALAYA & OTHER COUNTRIES

ANNAPURNA TREKKERS GUIDE

EVEREST - A TREKKER'S GUIDE

LANGTANG, GOSAINKUND & HELAMBU A Trekker's Guide

MOUNTAIN WALKING IN AFRICA 1: KENYA

OZ ROCK - A Rock Climber's guide to Australian Crags

ROCK CLIMBS IN HONG KONG

TREKKING IN THE CAUCAUSUS

ADVENTURE TREKS IN NEPAL

ADVENTURE TREKS - WESTERN NORTH AMERICA

CLASSIC TRAMPS IN NEW ZEALAND

GENERAL OUTDOOR BOOKS

THE ADVENTURE ALTERNATIVE

ENCYCLOPAEDIA OF MOUNTAINEERING

FAMILY CAMPING

FAR HORIZONS - Adventure Travel for All!

THE TREKKER'S HANDBOOK

FIRST AID FOR HILLWALKERS

THE HILLWALKERS MANUAL

LIMESTONE -100 BEST CLIMBS IN BRITAIN

MOUNTAIN WEATHER

SNOW & ICE TECHNIQUES

ROPE TECHNIQUES IN MOUNTAINEERING

CANOEING

CANOEIST'S GUIDE TO THE NORTH EAST

SNOWDONIA WILD WATER, SEA & SURF

WILDWATER CANOEING

CARTOON BOOKS IDEAL GIFTS

ON FOOT & FINGER

ON MORE FEET & FINGERS

LAUGHS ALONG THE PENNINE WAY

THE WALKERS

A full range of guidebooks to walking - short walks, family walks, long distance treks, scrambling, ice-climbing, rock climbing, and other adventurous pursuits worldwide

Other guides are constantly being added to the Cicerone List.
Available from bookshops, outdoor equipment shops or direct (send for price list)
from CICERONE, 2 POLICE SQUARE, MILNTHORPE, CUMBRIA, LA7 7PY

CICERONE GUIDES

Cicerone publish a wide range of reliable guides to walking and climbing worldwide

FRANCE, BELGIUM & LUXEMBOURG

THE BRITTANY COASTAL PATH

CHAMONIX MONT BLANC - A Walking Guide

THE CORSICAN HIGH LEVEL ROUTE: GR20

FRENCH ROCK

THE PYRENEAN TRAIL: GR10

THE RLS (Stevenson) TRAIL

ROCK CLIMBS IN BELGIUM & LUXEMBOURG

ROCK CLIMBS IN THE VERDON

TOUR OF MONT BLANC

TOUR OF THE OISANS: GR54

TOUR OF THE QUEYRAS

TOUR OF THE VANOISE

WALKING IN THE ARDENNES

WALKING THE FRENCH ALPS: GR5

WALKING IN HAUTE SAVOIE

WALKING IN THE TARENTAISE & BEAUFORTAIN ALPS

WALKING THE FRENCH GORGES (Provence)

WALKS IN VOLCANO COUNTRY (Auvergne)

THE WAY OF ST JAMES: GR65

FRANCE / SPAIN

WALKS AND CLIMBS IN THE PYRENEES

ROCK CLIMBS IN THE PYRENEES

SPAIN & PORTUGAL

WALKING IN THE ALGARVE

ANDALUSIAN ROCK CLIMBS

BIRDWATCHING IN MALLORCA

COSTA BLANCA CLIMBS

MOUNTAIN WALKS ON THE COSTA BLANCA

ROCK CLIMBS IN MAJORCA, IBIZA & TENERIFE

WALKING IN MALLORCA

THE MOUNTAINS OF CENTRAL SPAIN

THROUGH THE SPANISH PYRENEES: GR11

WALKING IN THE SIERRA NEVADA

WALKS & CLIMBS IN THE PICOS DE EUROPA

THE WAY OF ST JAMES: SPAIN

SWITZERLAND including adjacent parts of France and Italy

THE ALPINE PASS ROUTE

THE BERNESE ALPS

CENTRAL SWITZERLAND

CHAMONIX TO ZERMATT The Walker's Haute Route

THE GRAND TOUR OF MONTE ROSA (inc Italy) 2 vols

WALKS IN THE ENGADINE

THE JURA - Walking the High Route and Winter Ski Traverses

WALKING IN TICINO

THE VALAIS - A Walking Guide

GERMANY / AUSTRIA / EASTERN & NORTHERN EUROPE

WALKING IN THE BAVARIAN ALPS

GERMANY'S ROMANTIC ROAD A guide for walkers and cyclists

HUT-TO-HUT IN THE STUBAI ALPS

THE HIGH TATRAS

KING LUDWIG WAY

KLETTERSTEIG - Scrambles

MOUNTAIN WALKING IN AUSTRIA

WALKING IN THE BLACK FOREST

WALKING IN THE HARZ MOUNTAINS

WALKING IN NORWAY

WALKING IN THE SALZKAMMERGUT

Ask for our catalogue which also shows our UK range of guidebooks to walking - short walks, family walks, long distance treks, scrambling, ice-climbing, rock climbing, and other adventurous pursuits.

Other guides are constantly being added to the Cicerone List.
Available from bookshops, outdoor equipment shops or direct (send for price list)
from CICERONE, 2 POLICE SQUARE, MILNTHORPE, CUMBRIA, LA7 7PY